From TRAUMA To
ABUNDANCE

Change Your Mind – Change Your World
Manifest Your Perfect Life

Sharon Dill
TraumaToAbundance.com

Sharon Dill
Johannesburg Hypnosis
4th Floor The Firs, Craddock Ave,
Johannesburg, South Africa 2196
(+27) 79 099 3252

www.TraumaToAbundance.com
www.JohannesburgHypnosis.co.za
www.HypnosisForCancer.co.za

Sharon Dill is available to speak at your business or conference event on a variety of topics. Call (+27) 79 099 3252 for booking information.

Change Your Mind – Change Your World!

Overcome Trauma & Manifest Your Dreams!

What would it be like if you could find the perfect manifesting technique? One that actually works for you?

Manifesting is a fascinating subject but getting it right can be a frustrating process. Sharon had the same problem. But she was determined to find the answers – and the answers, when she found them, surprised even her!

You see, manifesting is not *'One Size Fits All'*. We all come from different backgrounds, have suffered various traumas, and have very different blocks, problems and limiting beliefs, all based on our individual experiences of the past.

The secret that Sharon stumbled onto is that manifesting is a very individual process. Everyone's journey is different!

In this book, Sharon shares her story and reveals her secrets. She takes you on a powerful journey of self-discovery, so you can decode, demystify, and understand manifesting, so you can transform your life.

Find the key to manifesting abundance for you, in your own way!

Are you ready to embrace lasting change?

You are more powerful than you could ever have imagined – all you need to do is open the door and step through!

Unlock Your Greatest Potential – The Ability to Manifest the Life of Your Dreams!

Discover How To:

- Transform Trauma
- Overcome Blocks
- Change Limiting Beliefs
- Learn to Program Your Mind
- Activate The Law of Attraction
- Create The Life of Your Dreams
- Step into Abundance, Love, Joy and Success!

Manifesting is a Real Thing, and Yes, It Does Work – If You Know How!

In this book, Sharon teaches you how!

Written by a Leading Expert with 10 Years' Experience

Sharon Dill is a SAIH Certified Professional Hypnotist and has been in private practice for over 10 years. She is an expert in helping people to transform their lives and create lasting success and abundance in all aspects of their lives. She has been interviewed on TV, and radio and her methods have been featured in magazines.

Sharon Dill is the expert other professionals come to, to become successful hypnotists themselves.

Since childhood, Sharon had a fascination with the question *"How Does The World Work?"* When she grew up, this interest transformed into finding out *"How Does Manifesting Work?"* Her determination to understand the process took her on a powerful journey from her own background of trauma into manifesting an abundant and richly rewarding life.

In this book, she shares her secrets and takes you on a journey to be able to manifest your dreams too.

Do you want Sharon Dill to be the motivational speaker at your next event? Call (+27) 79 099 3252 or visit TRAUMATOABUNDANCE.COM

Acknowledgements

I would like to acknowledge and thank the following people:

Thomas Budge – My teacher and mentor. Thank you for your wisdom and insights, as well as your passion for hypnosis. You are an inspiration!

Claudia Klein and SAIH – Your hypnosis methods are amazing and powerful and equipped me with a wonderful tool to help many people. Thank you also, for helping me to heal the past and open a door which has led to so much joy and fulfilment in my career and personal life.

Meagan – My daughter and editor, who tirelessly helped me knock this book into shape! Thank you for your love, dedication, advice and support.

Sandra – My daughter, for her wisdom, courage, love and support. You are amazing!

And to Grace – my granddaughter, who is smart, quirky, fun, and makes me laugh!

Table of Contents

PART ONE

INTRODUCTION

CHAPTER ONE

My Journey - The Awakening

The Beginning

For many years, in fact, since I was nine, I wondered how to Make Things Happen. Being a curious child, I liked to think about things. My questions were endless and drove my parents crazy! But I wanted to know...how does the world work?

I remember one particularly sweltering day, driving home with my stepfather. At the time we lived on a farm and driving to school and back was an hour-long trip on dirt roads in the scorching African heat. In those days, only fancy expensive cars had aircon, and the heat in the car was almost unbearable.

Sometimes my Stepfather would stop and buy us a cold drink. But not often. Most days, he would simply drive past the shop... and it was a lesson. My stepfather was all about lessons. You see, if I asked for something, it was Bad Manners, and I was punished. I would most definitely not get that cooldrink by asking.

You see, my stepfather was A Gentleman. A Very British Gentleman and Manners were Everything.

On one particularly hot afternoon, I started fantasizing about that cool drink. The taste of it, in my mouth; the ice-cold liquid running down my throat... The icy glass bottle... I could almost see the ice-cold droplets on the outside of the bottle, and feel the coolness of the melting drops on my hands...

And then it happened... magically! The car slowed down and he pulled into the parking lot, went inside, and bought us that deliciously icy cold drink. At the time, I was dumbstruck! I can remember thinking, 'It's so easy to make something happen... What fun!'

Looking back now, I'm grateful to him... because not being allowed to ask, forced me to dig deeper to get my cold drink on that day.

But the fact that I was not allowed to ask for things was a double-edged sword. It instilled in me a negative belief system that took decades to overcome: *I am not allowed to ask for anything.*

But it also drew my attention to something really interesting: I Can *Make Things Happen* (Sometimes). The problem was it

SHARON DILL

didn't always work. I can remember our family visiting friends' homes and they served Crème Brulé for dessert. Crème Brulé is traditionally served in ramekins (which are tiny bowls). That one tiny ramekin of Crème Brulé was delicious, but not nearly enough for a nine-year-old! I wanted another bowl so badly, but I never asked because it was *Bad Manners!* On that occasion, I didn't have an extra serving of Crème Brulé and I couldn't make it happen.

Of course, as a child, my focus was on other, *More Important Things*. Playing in the river, riding my bike on dirt roads, chickens and eggs, cows, sheep, and goats that would put their little heads down and butt you, if you turned your back, ducks that liked to swim in our swimming pool, rafts to build so we could float down the river... Life was fun!

Making Things Happen was quite low on my list of Important Things To Do.

But life wasn't all sunshine and roses when I was a child. There was also a lot of trauma. My real father had adored me in the five years my parents were together. I had, quite literally, been the apple of his eye, the adored child, the centre of his Universe. But when my parents divorced, he walked out of my life as if I no longer existed. I had been abandoned, thrown aside like a rag doll. Unwanted.

The effect of being abandoned by my father who had previously loved me so deeply caused more conflict in my mind. And, as children do, I blamed myself. It was my fault...

there was something wrong with me. This caused another limiting belief: *I am unlovable.*

But I distracted myself with farm life. I loved being on the farm... the animals, the sense of adventure... It was fun.

But my brief glimmer of happiness on the farm was snatched away from me at the age of six when I was sent away to boarding school. Being sent to boarding school compounded my feelings of abandonment and worthlessness. It was a dark period in my life. I felt as if I didn't exist.

This caused a third limiting belief: *Nothing good ever lasts.*

I now had three deep-set limiting beliefs:

- I am not allowed to ask for anything

- I am unlovable

- Nothing good ever lasts

These beliefs caused huge problems later in my life. By the age of 45, I had made a lot of bad choices and a lot of mistakes, and my life reflected the chaos... It was a crazy mess. I had two divorces and a string of abusive and failed relationships. Even worse, I seemed to attract drama and problems wherever I went.

But I wanted change... desperately. At the time, The Secret had just been published, and The Law Of Attraction became popular. So, I turned my attention back to *Making Things*

Happen. I was determined that I was going to manifest *the perfect life.*

So, I signed up for the courses, read the books, and did the affirmations and visualisations. And failed miserably. Manifesting my perfect life and creating the life of my dreams was not as simple as it seemed.

But my failure to manifest anything of significance didn't stop the questions in my mind... why? Why did others get such great results, while my life continued to be a miserable mess? Why was it that everywhere I went, I attracted problems, while others seemed to succeed at manifesting amazing lives with great ease? What was wrong with me?

I remember standing in a shop one day, paying for an item I had just purchased. At the time fate had just dealt me yet another hard blow and I was reeling... the house I was renting had burned down, along with most of my possessions.

The lady behind the counter was a friend, and one look at my face told her that something was very wrong. She sat me down with a cup of tea and held my hand as my problems spilled out of my mouth: all the misfortune I seemed to attract, the string of abusive relationships, the sheer bad luck... the house I was living in had recently burned to the ground... She shook her head in disbelief.

Seeing the shock on her face was a wake-up call, and for a moment I saw myself through her eyes. At that moment I understood something that had previously eluded me: *this is not normal. Other people don't have these kinds of problems!*

My mind ran over my most recent failed relationship. He had a temper, and I was afraid, but some part of me enjoyed making him angry. So, I provoked him. I realise now that I felt so helpless in the relationship, that the only power I had was to make him angry.

I spent nights sobbing on the couch in the living room, hopeless and alone. I thought my tears would make him care, but my misery had the opposite effect on him. He enjoyed seeing me helpless and in pain, as much as I enjoyed making him angry.

Now, sitting opposite my friend, and observing my patterns objectively for the first time in my life, I knew I had caused at least some of these problems. I had made bad choices. I had said yes to abuse and allowed my partners to take over my life and control me... I could not go on like this! I had to do something!

My first step was to face the fact that I had allowed these abusive men into my life in the first place. As I examined the reasons for my poor choices, I realised that I was desperate for love, and terribly afraid of being alone; in fact, it was blatantly obvious that I would put up with anything, rather than be alone.

Further analysis revealed that attracting emotionally unavailable men was one of my patterns. And it went right back to my father's abandonment. In some twisted way, I was trying to prove that I was worthy of love… that if I could get someone emotionally unavailable to want me and show me, unconditional love, then I would somehow 'win'. I would prove I was worth something; that I wasn't unlovable.

Taking a good hard look at myself, I realised just how unhealthy my relationships were, and I resolved right then and there, to change. So, I went in search of answers.

My search for information on dysfunctional relationships led me to a book on co-dependency. I had heard the phrase co-dependency, but I had never thought of it in the context of my messy relationships. Reading the book helped me to understand why I did the things I did, and I found the strength to make a powerful commitment to myself to remain single for two full years.

It seemed like a daunting task, and I was terrified. I had never been alone. Since 13, I had been in a continuous stream of relationships with hardly a breath between… No wonder my relationships were a mess!

Staying single wasn't easy. There were times when I was so restless and anxious that I paced the floor, back and forth, back and forth, willing myself to do what was good for me, instead of what I wanted to do. But I did it. And in those two years, I finally started to find my feet. I came to realise that real love came from inside, not outside. I read another book about being single.

The book spoke about finding balance, about not putting all your eggs into one basket. As I read the book, I realised that I had built my entire life around trying to keep my partners happy. I sacrificed everything and put all my energy into each new successive relationship. And every time a relationship fell apart, so did my entire world. And each time my world fell apart, I would rush out and find a new relationship.

Being single was a whole new experience. I began to develop interests and hobbies. I became sociable, and outgoing and developed friendships. I started to live. Life became fun and fulfilling. And I scoured the library for interesting topics to read about.

One day, I stumbled onto a book on hypnosis and was fascinated. I took the book home, devoured it, and recorded my voice. When I played back the recording, I got goosebumps... I could hardly believe the calm, tranquil, beautiful voice was mine! I found a hypnosis school and called them to find out more. Coincidentally the owner of the school answered the phone. *'You have a great voice for hypnosis,'* she told me. It was an affirmation, and my heart sang! I had found my calling!

Studying hypnosis was fascinating, absorbing and fun. And as I progressed through the courses, there was a wonderful side effect... I began to feel better about life. I and my fellow students needed practice, so we practised on each other, and I got a lot of 'free' hypnotherapy.

My depression, low self-esteem, mood swings, and intense fear and distrust of the world started to subside. I began to observe the process of my inner healing, and it fascinated me. The human mind and how it worked became my favourite subject, and I observed and studied others as avidly as I studied myself. Hypnosis and the study of the human mind also reawakened an old interest: The Law of Attraction.

Once again, I started reading the manifesting books and doing the affirmations. I visualised myself looking and feeling successful, but still with very limited results.

One good thing in my life was that, despite my messy personal life, I had applied myself at work and over the years had very successfully climbed the corporate ladder. Along the way, I discovered that I was an achiever. It was a wonderful surprise and I loved that about myself.

But even though I had done well at work and was earning a good salary, the commitment to being single made things financially tough. I barely made my budget each month… Apart from paying the rent, and feeding and clothing my daughter and myself, I was also putting my daughter through university. The hypnosis courses cost a bomb too.

So, understandably, my focus was on money… or rather, the lack of it. This fuelled an intense fear that I would never be able to switch from my well-paid corporate job to having a full-time hypnotherapy practice. And it didn't help that everyone in my life… my family and friends, fellow students, work colleagues… Everyone kept reminding me that *"Hypnosis is not a job. You can't expect to earn a living from being a hypnotist. And whatever you do, don't give up your day job!"*

I was distraught. How on earth was I going to make the transition from being employed and earning a corporate salary to having a full-time successful and lucrative hypnosis practice? The responsibility of my daughter's studies lay heavy on my mind. There was no way I would jeopardise her future. It's not like I could quit my job and take six months to a year to start my business… I just didn't have that luxury. The chasm between where I was and where I wanted to be yawned in front of me, seemingly impossible to breach. I had no idea how I was going to do it.

For a while, I was really depressed. And frustrated. And angry. And I didn't know what to do or how to do it to achieve my goal.

As for manifesting, that clearly wasn't working for me. My happiness, a decent bank balance and the chance to practice hypnosis all seemed elusive, like a distant dream. Someone else's distant dream. It was so frustrating!

It all came to a head in my final year of hypnosis study. I had just qualified, and I can remember complaining to a friend one evening, bewailing the hopelessness of my situation…

'I hate my job, and I don't like the people there. I'm so frustrated and bored! I can't do this anymore!'

Her answer shook me to the core: *"Nothing will change until you stop resisting your present circumstances... What you resist, persists..."*

At that moment, it felt as if my heart shattered into a million pieces. I was devastated. Didn't she understand how hard it was, how much I'd been through? The devastation was quickly followed by red hot anger as I outright rejected her words. It could not be true!

As I drove home that night, her words echoed in my mind: *'What you resist persists...'* How, then, was I ever to break free, I questioned. Surely, in order to change something, you need to push against it... reject it? It made no sense to me at all!

'This is rubbish... Nonsense!' I ranted all the way home. *'She doesn't know what I've been through! Don't I also deserve some happiness?'*

At the time, I was desperately frustrated at work. Although I was at the corporate level, there were politics... a lot of office politics... and I was so over it! The drama seemed petty, shallow and insignificant in comparison to becoming a hypnotist.

I had also become bored with my job and my achievements. Early in my career, I'd been promoted from data capture to the accounting department. Back then, it was an incredible

- 21 -

challenge, and it was fun to apply myself and climb the corporate ladder without so much as a degree. But now I was bored. I had gone as far as I wanted to go in accounting. I needed a new challenge. And hypnosis was that challenge. I craved being able to open my practice and go into business for myself.

So, there I was, unhappy and unfulfilled in my job. I was a fully qualified hypnotist, but unable to make the move into a full-time practice.

So, when I went out that night and my friend told me: *"You need to let go of wanting the change so badly, and you need to accept the situation that you are in. You've got to stop resisting… the more you resist, the more it persists …"* It was the last thing I wanted to hear!

How could accepting the situation change anything, I questioned. It didn't make sense. How was I ever going to escape my circumstances? Accepting the situation would surely mean that I would be stuck there. Forever… The thought was horrifying, and I rejected it with every shred of my being.

But by the next morning I had cooled down and her words got me thinking… And as I pondered the state of my life, I realised how much fear there was about not having any money to start my hypnosis practice… and how angry I had been when driving home the previous night…

I started thinking about manifesting…. and I remembered that every manifesting book I had ever read said that negative emotions blocked the flow of abundance. And for the third time in my life, I turned my attention to manifesting. Was it possible that my fear, my anger and my frustration with the situation was actually blocking me from manifesting my dreams?

And as I started to observe myself and my patterns, I realised how negative and obsessed I'd become. Everything was serious. I hardly laughed anymore. All my focus was on the misery in my life.

'Poor me… Everyone else has things so easy,' I thought to myself. And at that moment, I realised that I was the one who was **creating my own misery.**

Was it possible that I was actually **manifesting negative things** in my life?

I had never heard of anyone manifesting negative things in their life before… The thought fascinated me. It was a different perspective.

Evaluating myself, I realised how heavy and dark my life had become, how depression and anger weighed me down. So, I decided to do a little experiment. I made a decision to lighten up… to take things less seriously. I made a conscious effort to stop being so negative, to stop criticisiticising and judging everything and everyone.

And I started playing with life… inventing new ways of lifting my spirit and quieting my mind. I experimented with my feelings, and my belief systems. But most of all, I became playful with life. I started to think of life as a game. Let's see what happens when I do this… And what happens when I do that…

Playing with different techniques shifted my mindset and my beliefs in a powerful way. The methods I used were new. The manifesting books taught other techniques, but none of them spoke of this. Unexpectedly, my new calm and positive mindset started to pay dividends. I began to feel better about life and about myself.

One technique, in particular, changed my outer world and my inner world, in only three days! Office politics began to subside, and where before there had been chaos and backstabbing and people actively causing problems for me, I had somehow manifested peace and cooperation. I was astounded!

Right there, I knew I was onto something important. If I could manifest such powerfully positive changes in my office environment so quickly, what else could I manifest? I was ecstatic and excited!

So, I started to play with other techniques. And continued to get amazing results.

It wasn't long before I turned my attention to playing with how to start my hypnosis practice. I had begun seeing clients at weekends and after hours, but I was still a long way from full-time practice. I loved every minute of it. I knew that I was born to help people and become a hypnotherapist!

Suddenly and unexpectedly, manifesting my own business started to escalate really quickly! Amazing coincidences and opportunities opened up right in front of me… it was almost as if I were being led by the hand and shown how to do this… like the chance meeting with a young man who knew all the info on how to create and design your own website, and how to optimize your site to get it to rise on Google search rankings. And the amazing thing was that he was running a course the following weekend!

I took his weekend course, went home, designed my website, and put it up. I put in extra research to understand Search Engine Optimization and watched in joy as my site rose through the rankings. Pretty soon, my site was on the first page… I was overjoyed. But it continued to rise even higher, and before long my site was at the very top of page one… the highest-ranked website for hypnosis in South Africa. And I wasn't even in full-time practice yet! I still had a day job!

It made me laugh so hard, that my stomach hurt… I couldn't believe it! It was crazy! But I was loving it, and I was filled with gratitude and joy.

In December when I took leave from my corporate job, my hypnosis practice was fully booked for the whole three weeks. When I went back to work in January, I was working two jobs! End of January, I gave my 30 days notice to quit my job.

End of Feb, I said goodbye forever to being employed.

March was my first month in full-time hypnosis practice, and I sailed through the month, easily reaching my target of matching my corporate salary. But that wasn't all... within two months of being in my brand-new practice, I was approached by a national magazine. They wanted to feature my weight loss program. I was thrilled. Could it get any better, I wondered. And it did... in that first year of being in full-time practice, I was approached to appear on TV, I was interviewed on radio and appeared in magazines. And the crazy thing was, I didn't go looking for them. They came to me!

Well, that's not entirely true... I did manifest the media attention with a simple thought. *'I wonder what it would be like to be on TV. Wouldn't that be fun!'*

It was like an awakening, the *'AHA, so that's how it's done,'* was so rewarding and so much fun!

But what was even more rewarding, was that I had stumbled onto these methods on my own! Not by taking the courses... although I think they helped me to understand the process. Not by repeating affirmations... I really don't like affirmations; they bore me to tears and make me feel frustrated! Not by visualisation... although, of all the techniques I had previously learned, this was the most valuable.

And as I continued to learn, observe, and play, life became a game. A richly rewarding, beautiful and exciting game!

One of the most interesting things I learned about manifesting is that it's a double-edged sword. Whatever your state of mind, good or bad, that is exactly what you will manifest in your life.

And as for the wonderful techniques, the finer details, the know-how of my methods, keep reading the next word, the next chapter, and all the way to the end. Each chapter is a step in preparing yourself, and laying the groundwork, to be able to successfully master the awesome Manifesting Techniques for yourself. In Chapter Ten, I spill the beans and give you a step-by-step process of exactly what I did that day and the days that followed, to manifest a powerful and magical life for myself.

So, if you would like to understand yourself better if you really want to learn to manifest, and if you truly want that beautiful life...keep reading... keep turning the pages of this awesome and fascinating book!

I think that one of the most misleading things in the manifesting books and courses is the belief that *'one size fits all.'* This is simply not true.

Manifesting is not a matter of *'one size fits all.'* It's definitely a very individual process. In this book, I will help you to manifest abundance, for you, in your way... because that's the only way it can work for you and your life.

You're in for the ride of your life! Abundance is your birthright, and by reading this book, you can claim it for yourself.

You deserve a good life... No, a great life!

Let's make this happen together.

CHAPTER TWO

The Law Of Negative Attraction

Why Do We Keep Attracting Negative Things Into Our Lives?

I am sitting opposite my new client, Paul. He is visibly upset.

"I can't believe this has happened again! Why does the same thing keep happening to me, over and over again?"

He has just explained how every time he achieves something great, it falls to pieces in front of his eyes. Not only does it fall to pieces, but something very specific that used to happen in his childhood seems to repeat itself… over and over again.

"I feel as if I'm stuck in a nightmare that never ends!"

Paul grew up in a very poor community, and there was hardly enough money to put food on the table. Clothes were handed down from child to child, and in his first year of school, he had to walk to school in the icy cold winter with no shoes and bare arms. Given these circumstances, one would think that perhaps scarcity and lack of money would be the problem. But it wasn't. He had done well for himself and had built a successful career, had bought his own lovely home and enough money in the bank for overseas holidays. So, no, money was not the issue.

It's interesting to note that sometimes the most obvious problems are not always the problems that manifest. The mind is a complex thing, and everyone processes things differently.

A deeper investigation revealed that when he was a child, his dad was an alcoholic, and regularly beat everyone in his family. And as sad and tough as that was, it still wasn't the issue.

He went on to explain that he had lived in a small community... and everyone knew everyone else's business. Consequently, the whole community knew about his dad's alcoholism, and the domestic violence, and people gossiped.

His family was mocked and laughed at, subject to pointing fingers and sniggers. The kids at school teased him and ridiculed his family for having an alcoholic and violent father. Being the laughingstock of the community cut him to the core and made for an extremely painful childhood.

When he grew up and went to university, he did exceptionally well. He is highly intelligent and got his degree easily, and he seemed set for life. When he started work, his excellence was recognised, and he was soon promoted and became the youngest manager in the company.

But his home life did not reflect his achievements at work. At first, things went well… he met a seemingly lovely girl, fell in love, got married and had children. And then the patterns from his childhood started reappearing. His wife became abusive and manipulative and constantly belittled him in front of friends and family. Again, just as in childhood, people gossiped and laughed behind his back.

Eventually, he got a divorce.

Being a young and single successful man, it wasn't long before he was in another relationship. This time it was a girl from the office. She seemed perfect, and before long they were married. But it wasn't long before the old patterns reappeared.

Once married she started to show her true colours and became manipulative, cruel and abusive. She taunted him in front of colleagues and set about destroying his career and his credibility. Once again people gossiped and talked.

Work became a nightmare. He lost confidence and became anxious. This made the problem worse; where once he was respected, now he was a victim of ridicule in the company.

"They treated me as if I was stupid," he told me. *"I'm not stupid. It was like my childhood all over again! Everyone was laughing at me behind my back…"*

Around this time his mother, with whom he was really close, passed away. His wife's response was to cause more trouble for him by gossiping with his family about how he had lost face at work. For the fourth time in his life, he was being ridiculed, this time by his own family.

It seemed that no matter what he did, the painful taunting reappeared over and over in his life.

Like Paul, you might have found yourself noticing some painful repeating patterns in your life too at some point or another. It's easy to start thinking, *'I **knew** this would happen! It **always** happens to me.'*

And we often compound the restrictions our mind places on us, by saying things like:

*'**People like me always get the short end of the stick…**'*

*'**I'm just not lucky in love…**'*

*'**Other people have all the luck…**'*

Or that famous saying, *'**The rich get richer, and the poor get poorer…**'*

I was watching a reality series recently about autistic young adults looking to find their perfect love match. One can imagine that being autistic makes finding love that much more complicated.

One of the contestants, Bradley, and his friend James were discussing love. *'The path of true love never did run smoothly,'* Bradley commented in a serious voice. Obviously, he was repeating something he'd either heard or been told. His friend James nodded his head sagely in agreement and I could see him absorbing and accepting this new information.

Later in that episode, James had a wonderful date with a lovely girl. You could see that they clicked. They had a lot of common interests and laughed and chatted and had a wonderful time together. But at the end of the date, James' face became sombre.

'You know what they say,' he blurted out, *'The path of true love never did run smoothly.'*

The girl's face fell. And that was pretty much the end of that relationship.

It was heartbreaking to watch James repeating, reinforcing and believing what Bradley had told him.

It is interesting to note here, that the subconscious mind cannot tell the difference between what is real and what is imagined. And maybe you are surprised to hear that, and you might even wonder how this could possibly be true.

Well, here's a little experiment: take a moment to imagine a big juicy lemon. Now cut it in half. Imagine feeling those little spurts of juice on the back of your hand, as you slice through the lemon. Next, cut it into quarters. Now take one of those quarters, and imagine bringing it to your mouth, and bite into that big juicy lemon! Feel that super sour juice running into your mouth. What happens? Your mouth starts producing saliva in response to the sour taste of the lemon - as if the lemon were real! So, the subconscious mind cannot tell the difference between what is real and what is imagined.

The funniest thing is that even though I have explained this concept hundreds of times to clients, every time I talk about this imaginary lemon, my mouth still produces saliva! One might think that after ten years in hypnosis practice, my subconscious mind would become accustomed to the 'imaginary' lemon! But no… apparently not!

Here's another example: think of a time when you heard a song on the radio and it instantly took you back in time to another time and another place, when you heard that song. Maybe you were on holiday, and suddenly it feels like you are there again, right now!

Even if I start to talk about imagining a beautiful sunny day on the beach, and how the sun feels on your skin, or if you prefer a walk in a cool shady forest, or swimming in a crystal-clear stream, or even lounging at the side of a swimming pool with an ice-cold drink in your hand… your mind is going to go there, and pretty soon it feels like you are there!

Do you see now? The subconscious mind does not understand the difference between what is real and what is imagined. The weird thing is that your conscious mind knows you are here, but your subconscious is simultaneously experiencing a very different reality.

So, I think we can agree that the subconscious mind cannot tell the difference between what is real, and what is imagined.

But the fact that the subconscious can't tell the difference between what is real and what is imagined, is a problem because when we believe something, good or bad, our subconscious mind totally accepts it without question. Not only does the subconscious mind accept and believe it, but it also actively sets about recreating that exact set of circumstances.

The more you accept the negative beliefs, the more entrenched they become in your mind. And the more entrenched they become in your mind, the more they become a permanent part of your life and actually become part of your reality. And the more they become part of your reality, the more you attract those same circumstances over and over again.

I wonder if you have ever found yourself trapped in repeating negative patterns in your life? And how helpless, desperate, and unhappy these patterns can make you feel. It feels as if you are out of control… hopeless and helpless to break free of the negative repeating patterns.

Sometimes the patterns are outer patterns, such as specific events which keep reappearing in your life.

Some examples of outer patterns are:

- Ending up in one disastrous job after another
- Attracting messy or abusive relationships
- Finding yourself in a bad situation not of your making
- Repeating negative circumstances which seem to pop up from nowhere
- Seeming to attract bad luck
- Being manipulated or bullied by people in your life, or at work
- Bearing the brunt of other people's bad behaviour
- Getting hurt over and over again

Sometimes the patterns are inner patterns, such as:

- Sabotaging a perfectly good relationship
- Messing up a fantastic job
- Turning down a golden opportunity

- Having limiting and fear-based thoughts such as, *'I'm just not good enough. They will find out I'm a fake. I'll never cope. I'll make mistakes and I'll end up being fired.'*

- Making bad decisions

These inner patterns can fall under the label of self-sabotage and can easily destroy our chances of happiness and success.

Then you get the patterns which are both inner and outer beliefs, where you find yourself repeating old patterns. I've had many clients who tell me things like:

'My father was an alcoholic. I always swore I would never marry an alcoholic. And then I went and married an alcoholic.'

Or *'My mother was manipulative and made me feel guilty about everything. I was blamed for every little thing and couldn't do anything right. Now my wife is manipulative and blames everything on me.'*

This is a perfect example of how our mind takes a snapshot of our circumstances, tells us this is a *'true version'* of the world, and sets about recreating it.

This is often compounded by things our parents tell us, which their parents told them, such as:

'Don't expect too much - you will be disappointed'

'People like us don't get to own fancy cars or live in big houses.'

'Men/women are only out to get you. You can't trust men/women.'

'Money is the root of all evil and brings no good.'

These beliefs cause problems in our psyche because as children we look to our parents for guidance as to how to interact with the world. Of course, as we grow older, we (hopefully) start to think for ourselves and can reject some of these outdated and false beliefs. But sometimes those things we were taught as children, stick. And we are often completely unaware of the repeating patterns in our life until we really start looking.

Childhood trauma also can play a huge part in predisposing us to recreate the exact same situations, over and over again. But in truth, this phenomenon of recreating painful circumstances is not only manifested from painful childhood experiences but can come from any traumatic or upsetting event, at any time in your life.

In fact, anything intensely painful can start a negative downward spiral and create what I call *The Law of Negative Attraction*. The mind takes a snapshot of a specific event, processes this information, and tells us, *'Based on the evidence of what happened in the past, this is what the future looks like too. This is what life is.'*

I recently saw a client who told me something really interesting:

'I taught myself to repel good things that come my way,' Sheila said.

Her story was very interesting. When she was young, her father started a marching band. Back then, marching bands were a big thing, and he travelled the world presenting his marching band troupe.

When Sheila was 20, her father invited her along on a trip to Asia. She had a wonderful time, and everyone loved her. The marching band caused a big fanfare in the country and everywhere they went, they were applauded and showered with gifts.

Being the daughter of the leader of the band, she, too, was showered with gifts. She was adored by the public and band members alike. She was even featured in the local newspaper: there was a big picture of her on the front page. Everyone made a fuss of her. She was even offered a scholarship to study further in the country.

But one of the band members, an older woman, was jealous of the attention she received and gave her a nickname: *'The Princess'*. The painful label upset Sheila and hit a nerve: she hated that she was getting all the attention on the merit of her father's success.

This prompted her to make a decision: *'I won't take anything that comes from my father.'* So, she turned down the scholarship and chose to make her own way in life.

A year later, she met and started dating a wealthy man who was a big spender. He showered her with expensive gifts.

Once again, she hated receiving the elaborate gifts, and once again it brought trouble into her life. Her friends became jealous and started bullying and mocking him, and his friends started bullying her. Once again, the gifts attracted jealousy and caused problems in her life. The relationship didn't last.

Since then, every time she is given a gift or receives something, it gets lost or broken or stolen …

'I'm so lucky,' she told me, *'I'm always getting gifts. But ever since that trip to Asia, something bad always happens to the things I'm given.'*

When she got married, Sheila's mother-in-law, who loved her deeply, gave her the family heirloom engagement ring. It was stolen when they moved house.

A good friend gifted her an expensive brooch… the first time she wore it, it fell off and was lost.

When a beloved uncle passed, Sheila inherited an antique desk she had always admired. During the move to bring the beautiful desk to her home, it started raining, and one side of the desk was exposed to the weather. As a result, it was ruined.

'Every time I get something nice,' she told me, *'Something happens to it. I'm jinxed! I repel gifts.'*

Once again strange and unnatural circumstances being repeated, over and over again. The circumstances in all of the above examples are just too strange and out there to be *just a coincidence'*. They are very specific and individual to the person involved.

This Law of Negative Attraction is a bit like a magnet that attracts more negativity, and in a very specific way. Each case is individual. Each case has its own set of negative repeating circumstances. The above are classic examples of The Law of Negative Attraction in action, as past circumstances repeat themselves over and over and over again.

In my own life, I have experienced many strange and repeating negative patterns. One of these was strangely related to a very specific time of year, from March to May. It seemed that during these months everything that could go wrong, would. Appliances broke, unexpected bad luck, drama, trouble and problems appeared in my life out of nowhere; one bad thing after another compounding the crushing feeling of *"Is this ever going to end?"*

With the result that every January and February, I found myself dreading the approaching month of March. I found myself filled with a feeling of fear gnawing at my guts. I would imagine that awful feeling of things going wrong, of being completely overwhelmed; the depression, the feeling that it would never end! I could feel the heaviness of the dark days ahead where it felt as if I were wading through deep dark scary fog with no end in sight.

This pattern repeated for many, many years. Each year I hoped that this year would be better. But it wasn't. I could not understand it. Being a keen observer of patterns, I realised there had to be a trigger, a cause…but what? I thought perhaps it was my parents' divorce when I was five years old… But it was the wrong time of the year. I was clueless.

It took many years to realise the cause of the pattern. One day, thinking about this pattern, I found my mind going back to my first marriage. In the beginning, it was great. I was young and in love and had been swept off my feet. For the first year, it was great fun being married. We lived close to my family, and there were lots of fun family times together.

But then my husband got a new job and we moved to the other side of the country. It was March. I remember the month very clearly because it was just after my son was born in February. After we moved, everything changed. Not because my son was born. But because my husband started to show his true colours. Now that I lived far from my family and was beyond their protective love, he became extremely cruel and abusive.

I can clearly remember the feeling of disappointment and heartbreak… the devastation of my hopes and dreams which lay in tatters at my feet. My mother had warned me about him and begged me not to marry him. I stubbornly hadn't listened. And now I was paying for it.

I endured his abuse for five long years before I found the courage to break away. But the memories of those months of misery, from March to May, the devastation of my dreams, my deep disappointment, and the feeling of being alone and in trouble. (I was much too proud to let my family know what was going on, and I definitely didn't want to let my mother know she had been right!)

After those three heart-breaking months, I adjusted and simply became numb. But long after I divorced him, the pain of those three months continued to haunt me, and with it came bad luck, things going wrong, depression, and a sense of hopelessness for three months of every year.

I must admit that when I realised the root of this pattern, it really surprised me. I truly thought I had completely resolved and worked through the trauma of my first marriage. And to a large degree, I had. But the sting of disappointment and the expectation of bad things to come in those three months of the year, long outlasted the actual trauma.

Isn't the mind an interesting thing?

Many people get stuck in The Law of Negative Attraction, or LONA as I like to call it. People find themselves reinforcing the negative patterns, such as:

'It's just the way my life is. I need to accept it.'

'I'm just unlucky. Bad things always happen to me.'

'There is no way out.'

People find themselves giving up, accepting and surrendering to their misery, as if it were a burden they were destined to carry. The sad part is that people often find it easier to accept the problems than try to change them.

Lessons In This Chapter

- What are the repeating patterns in your life? Where is LONA active? Make a list of repeating negative patterns which appear in your life. Where did they come from? What is it about? Write down your thoughts and insights, so you can get a clear picture of what's going on, and why.

- Have you seen LONA with its negative loops and repeating patterns in other people's lives? List those and add any thoughts or insights you might have about those.

Remember, we are studying LONA, which includes noticing patterns everywhere we see them, ours or others. But also, a word of caution. Please don't rush in to inform people about their negative patterns. You are not here to fix other people. And unless someone specifically asks for help, they are unlikely to appreciate your assessment of their life.

You are also not here to judge others or their patterns. It's just a way to train your mind to observe patterns, wherever they appear.

Focussing on other people's problems is a trap by the way. Many people distract themselves from their own problems by spending their time and energy on other people's problems.

In this way, they avoid taking responsibility for their own problems.

You are here to help you, and part of helping you is to notice and study patterns in others too… objectively, with non-judgement and empathy. So, observe the patterns with a sense of detachment and perhaps curiosity. After all, the human mind and its patterns are fascinating!

And don't be hard on yourself when you find your patterns. Remember: none of us is perfect. And frankly who wants to be? Life is just interesting and cool and full of information. But it can be better – a whole lot better!

You can have a wonderful life… if you know how!

So, is your life set in stone? The answer to that is simple: *only if you believe it is!*

There is a way to escape LONA. You are not trapped. Life is not a Done Deal. If there's one thing I've learned, it's that **Life is a Work in Progress.**

So yes, you absolutely can break free of LONA. I know because I've done it, and I'm going to teach you how to do it for yourself too.

CHAPTER THREE

Change Your Mind And You Change Your Life

Your Mind Is A Frequency Transmitter

Understanding the way your mind processes information is key to changing your thought processes. You need to change the way you think, to start having control over your life and destiny. Noticing your patterns is a good place to start.

I had an interesting experience that, even though it was a relatively small matter, demonstrated The Law Of Attraction very clearly.

I've always enjoyed driving. I grew up driving on dirt roads on the farm, and because of that, I'm a very good driver! But I haven't always been the most patient driver. Although I wouldn't say that I had road rage, I was definitely prone to outbursts of anger and frustration about bad drivers. And of course, I seemed to attract all the worst drivers!

One day while driving home, a taxi driver darted out unexpectedly in front of me. I was forced to slam on my brakes to avoid a collision. I blasted him with my hooter, but he drove off as if nothing had happened. I was fuming! It put me in a foul mood the rest of the drive home.

As I parked my car, I sat for a moment to catch my breath. Why did I attract so many bad drivers? It was insane! That taxi has almost caused an accident!

But then, like a bolt of lightning, it hit me.

'Sharon,' I said out loud, *'Haven't you learned yet? Don't you know the more you believe there are so many bad drivers out there, the more bad drivers you will attract!'*

I laughed out loud at my foolishness. But right there I made a decision. I made a conscious effort to start thinking different thoughts and feeling different things about driving.

Every time I went out, I would say things like: *'There are so many good drivers on the road… Everyone is so courteous… People let me in whenever I need a gap… And the taxi drivers… Well… I understand that they are just trying to reach their daily quotas to earn a living, so I'm going to give them space to get to where they need to go.'*

And so, filled with my new instilled beliefs about drivers, if I came across a bad driver, I made a point of shrugging it off: '*I guess he's in a hurry to get somewhere…*'

And guess what? The bad drivers started to disappear! I started attracting the most courteous drivers; the best drivers; drivers who gave me a gap when I needed it.

A couple of weeks later, the strangest thing happened. It was peak hour traffic, and I was battling to get across a lane of traffic which was backed up over the bridge and out of sight. The fact that it was rush hour meant, of course, that everyone was in a hurry to get home. I waited patiently for someone to give me a gap, and he did, guess who it was? A taxi driver! He waved me across with a cheerful wave, and as I waved back to thank him, I knew I had changed my pattern! It felt great!

When we change our thoughts, we change our world. It's that simple.

An interesting thing happened last week, which showed me that I have truly shifted this previous negative pattern. I was stuck in traffic again, four lanes of traffic backed up solid, as far as the eye could see. I noticed the left lane starting to move a bit faster, as traffic jams sometimes do, and I thought '*I would love a gap to be able to move over…*' Instantly, within the blink of an eye, a space opened, and it wasn't just a small space… it was literally five car lengths! And I was able to move over into the faster lane easily and safely.

Then I noticed the lane on the left was again moving very quickly. Being well aware that I manifested the previous gap, I playfully thought, *'I wonder if I can do that again… I'd love a gap…'* And again, in a split second, another five-car gap opened, and I was able to move across into the fastest lane.

The interesting thing about it was, that it wasn't just a small gap… both times it was a huge gap. It's so interesting to note these things, and they raise so many questions. How come the other cars behind me didn't take the gap? Did no one else see the gap? Why didn't they see it? How did the gap open up so quickly? I had hardly thought the thought when the gap appeared… not once, but twice! It was like magic!

It still boggles my mind how quickly the gap appeared… literally seconds after I thought, *'I'd love a gap,'* my desire manifested itself. This is an indication of how fast the Law Of Attraction and manifesting can work!

Isn't it amazing how powerful it is to change your belief systems? And that's what this book is all about… changing your beliefs about the way the world works. Because, changing what you believe about the world and about yourself, literally changes your world!

How does manifesting work?

The first thing to understand is that the human mind is a frequency transmitter, very much like a radio transmitter.

Only it's a two-way transmitter. The signal you transmit or send out, is exactly what comes back to you.

Transmitting, or sending out signals, is very much like going to a restaurant and deciding what to order. You can order anything you like on the menu. The waiter is not going to argue with your choice. He's simply going to go to the kitchen, place your order, and bring your food when it is ready.

So, my question is… would you order fries, if you hate fries? No. And when the fries that you ordered arrived at your table, would you blame the waiter for your choice? No. So why then are we so surprised and angry when we manifest bad stuff for ourselves, by being negative? By having negative belief systems, you are automatically placing an order for more negativity to appear in your life. It's that simple.

The Universe / God / Your Higher Self or whatever you believe in, responds directly to your mindset and the signals you transmit. By focusing on something, whether it be good or bad, you are placing an order with The Universe, so naturally, that is exactly what you will get.

(I'm going to use 'The Universe' in this book for ease of reference, but you can substitute any higher power or anything else with which you are comfortable.)

It, therefore, follows that you cannot manifest good things from a place of fear, worry or emotional pain. The conundrum is that in order to manifest good things, we need to feel secure, safe, happy and validated. But how do we achieve that powerful state of mind, when our actual physical experience of life is an experience of lack, unhappiness, insecurity and emotional pain? Added to that is the pressure of daily life, meeting our children's needs, meeting deadlines at work, obligations, financial problems, stress and worry.

With all this going on in our lives, our own needs often end up last on the list, as we stumble from one crisis to the next, barely coping. But in reality, the fact that you are putting everyone else's needs above your own is where the problem actually starts. You need to put your own needs above anything else in your life. It can be no other way.

Now I know that we have all been taught that self-sacrifice is honourable, and it is often expected of us. The pressure we put ourselves last is a burden which has been handed down through the generations. Women have been taught to be submissive and hold back, to put their family's needs before their own. Men are pressured to provide for their families, often having to work long hours, sacrificing family time, health and personal needs. We have been taught and schooled to serve others before ourselves, to such an extent that putting time and energy into ourselves can make us feel selfish and guilty.

Thank goodness this is changing… and it needs to! The world is shifting, and we are all waking up to the fact that the Old

Ways need to go, to make way for a more fulfilled and joyful way of living so that the whole world can benefit.

Prioritizing yourself is not a selfish act. It is an act of great generosity to you and everyone in your life. I think that we are becoming aware that when we are happy, we make the people around us happy too. So, everyone wins.

And if you feel good about yourself, and you feel fulfilled and excited about life, you are going to be better at everything in your life... a better mother and spouse, more productive and focused in your career, a better friend, and, although this may sound contrary, you will have more energy too. Everything is better.

You might ask how it is possible to have more energy when you are accomplishing more and doing more. The answer is really simple. Negative emotions and states such as fear, anger, anxiety, and insecurity, literally suck the energy out of us. Think of how exhausted you feel after an ordeal... Or how drained you feel when things are constantly going wrong. Negative emotions are exhausting!

It, therefore, stands to reason that in order to have more energy, we need to resolve our problems and find a more positive and peaceful way to operate in the world.

But if trauma, emotional pain, scarcity and lack, has been your experience in life, how do you overcome the resulting limiting beliefs, and the deep sense of guilt when you do things for yourself? How do you let go of the fear that these beliefs have instilled in your mind? How do you start to trust life and people, when you've been hurt and abused?

This takes us back to that negative loop... how do we resolve our pain, anger, fear and frustration, so that we can manifest great things in our lives? Where do we even start?

Well, the good news is that I did it, I made the transition, so I'm going to show you how you can do it too.

Change your mind and you change your world

So where do we start? You might feel overwhelmed at this seemingly huge task, but I'm going to take you through the process, step by step. We are going to break this down into bite-sized pieces so that you can progress from a state of unfulfilled yearning to a life of abundant joy.

YOUR PAST CREATES YOUR FUTURE
Understand Your Mind - Why Does It Manifest Negative Events?

Understanding your own mind and how it works, goes at the top of the list of actions to bring about inner change. You see, until you can begin to unravel the riddle of your mind, your past will continue to create your future. The sad thing is the more trauma and pain in your past, the more likely you are to expect more bad things to happen in the future too. And it's not surprising. Trauma, emotional pain, disappointments, and betrayals can easily affect the way we feel about people, the world, and ourselves.

Let's face it, it's not easy to feel safe and at ease in life (so that you can manifest good things), when you don't feel safe or at ease.

So, in Chapter Four, I expand on how the mind works, so you can fully understand the process of why, when you have been through trauma and problems, your mind continues to recreate these patterns.

The beauty of it is when you understand your mind, you can also understand how to break free from these repeating patterns.

HEAL THE PAST
What You Are Holding Onto, Is Holding You Back!

Once you understand your mind, healing the past comes next in Chapter Five. And healing the past is all about learning to let go of your stuff. Holding onto stuff is like holding onto a hot coal. If your fist is closed tightly around that hot coal, and you refuse to let it go, how do you expect to be able to receive anything? Receiving requires open hands, not hands locked in a fist held tight in anger and hate. And this may seem like a simplistic explanation, but I can assure you that it is 100% true.

The bottom line is, that anything you are holding onto, is holding you back. Even if you are desperately trying to send out signals of abundance and joy to The Universe, the desperation in your signals means you are sending mixed messages. The result will, at best, be mixed results.

When I started working with manifesting, I sent out signals of yearning and longing, unhappiness and desperation. The only thing it brought me was more things to make me feel more unhappy, sad and desperate.

HEAL THE NOW
Handling Difficulties In Life With Ease

Once you have set yourself free from the past, it's time to heal The Now. In Chapter Six I talk about how healing The Now is all about the ability to handle present circumstances and difficulties with ease.

You might start by asking yourself, *'Who am I? And how do I process life? How do I cope with stressful events and problems?'*

These are hard questions, and you might not like the answers. But the ability to remain calm and in control under stressful conditions is key to being able to manifest the life you want. The first step to being in control of your world is to be in control of yourself.

Now I know this is not easy and can seem like a tall order, but in order to shift into abundance and joy, you need to find a way to handle your problems in a more constructive way.

I know and empathize with you and what you are going through, because I've been there myself, and I found the way out, and I'm going to help you to find the way out too.

I've walked the walk and talked the talk, and I learned and understood. Now I'm going to help you understand too, so that you, too, can start to feel more in control of your life.

And when you feel more in control, manifesting comes easily.

GETTING OUT OF YOUR OWN WAY
Break Away From Fear

One of the biggest obstacles to manifesting is ourselves. We can be our own worst enemy. We are all individual human beings, and how we react to various situations is as individual as we are.

Sometimes, we are completely unaware of how we block ourselves, and one of the biggest blocks in life is fear. Surprisingly, all of our problems and negative emotions actually stem from fear. Fear is a base emotion. And it is a powerful negative force, which can easily derail your efforts to break free from the past.

In Chapter Seven, we delve deeper into the mind to understand the role of fear, so that we can learn to release the fear, and get out of our own way.

LEARN TO LOVE YOU AND LIKE YOU
Be Your Own Best Friend!

Once you have let go of the past and are in control of the present, and have gotten out of your own way, the next step is to start liking and loving who you are. In chapter eight I talk about the importance of liking you and loving you.

The bottom line is that you are not going to be able to manifest if you don't love yourself and like yourself.

You need to value yourself to feel deserving of good things. And when you feel deserving of good things you will be able to manifest your desires easily.

LEARN TO PROGRAM YOUR MIND
Take Control Of Your World

Chapter Nine deals with taking control of your inner thought processes. Think of your mind like a garden: if you want a beautiful garden, you prepare the soil, you plant the seeds, and you water them. When the seeds start to sprout, you nurture them, fertilize them and tend to your garden every day with love and care. You look out for invasive weeds and pull them out before they overrun your garden.

Tending to the mind is exactly like that, and here I give lots of ways for you to work with your mind, to start expecting good things to happen in your life.

CHANGE YOUR MIND AND YOU CHANGE YOUR WORLD
The Beginning: Getting It Right

In Chapter Ten, I spill the beans, give you the know-how, and share my secrets. Here I tell my story of exactly what I did and how I did it, to manifest the most magical things for myself. I share how I started getting my mind to work for me, instead of against me.

One of the most magical things I discovered on my journey, is that you don't even need to know what you want, to manifest it. This had been one of the things which had previously blocked me from being able to manifest. You see, when you are living in trauma, it's extremely difficult to imagine a good life, never mind what exactly that good life would look like!

But I found ways to overcome that block, which left me feeling blessed, secure, protected and joyful, and brought the exact things I needed to move to the next level, without me even needing to know what those things were.

It was almost as if The Universe took stock of my situation and said, *'In order to succeed, you will need this, and this, and this...'* And then proceeded to conjure them all up for me, without me lifting a finger! How's that for magic?!

How would you like to conjure some magic of your own? Manifesting really is magic in action. And I am a living testimony to that.

LET'S MAKE IT HAPPEN
Fall In Love With Life And Life Will Fall In Love With You

In Chapter Eleven, I discuss and expand on the many ways you can start manifesting and get results.

Here we learn to play with techniques and how to achieve powerful states of mind for manifesting. I give easy exercises to help you train your brain, so you can manifest in a fun, easy and very effective way.

I also share great ways to design your mantras and affirmations – the right and wrong ways of structuring your wording, what works and what doesn't, so you can create your own affirmations and mantras which will work for you.

GETTING THE VERY BEST OUT OF YOUR LIFE
Transform Yourself - Transform Your World!

In Chapter Twelve, I give step-by-step instructions on how to transform negative beliefs into new powerful thought patterns which work for you. Here we discuss changing limiting beliefs about money, love, career, business, as well as reframing beliefs such as *'Nothing good can last'*, and *'Money doesn't grow on trees'* and *'Unlucky in Love.'*

Did you know that manifesting is not only something you learn but that you can actually train your brain to manifest things for you? So, in this chapter I give manifesting exercises you can practice in your daily life, to get your brain to get into the habit of being able to manifest the things you desire.

I also share amazing techniques for manifesting specific desires, by teaching you how to manipulate time and emotions.

CONCLUSION:

So, is manifesting only for the privileged, or the smart, or the lucky? No, absolutely not! The truth is that the Law Of Attraction and Manifesting is one of the greatest puzzles on this earth, and I believe we were destined to solve this puzzle.

Understand this. You were born to find the answers to unlocking happiness and abundance in every part of your life. Obstacles were never meant to block you... they were meant to teach you about life, to make you wise and strong and amazing so you could get out there and fulfil your destiny, whatever that is for you as an individual. You were born to overcome, to rise above, and to become more!

Happiness and abundance is your birthright, and it's yours for the taking. All you have to do is open your hands, your arms, and your heart, and press the Receive Button.

PART TWO

THE JOURNEY

CHAPTER FOUR

*Your Past Creates
Your Future*

Understand Your Mind - Why Does It Manifest Negative Events?

Have you ever noticed that when things start to go wrong, everything goes wrong? It almost seems as if one small incident can spiral out of control very quickly into a mass of problems, like a huge ball rolling down a hill, gathering speed as it goes, with us watching helplessly as it smashes everything in its path on the way down.

And the more things spiral out of control, the more angry/fearful we become, which somehow seems to escalate the entire issue and create yet more problems. And eventually, at some point, it all stops as suddenly as it started, and life seems to return to normal.

The interesting thing is that if you look at the patterns and timing of these difficult times, then you might begin to understand what is really going on... that what happens in your life is truly a mirror image of how you were feeling at the time when the problems first started.

The truth is that the more negative, fearful and miserable you are feeling, the more problems you are likely to attract in life. So, we can begin to connect the dots and understand that the more difficulties and trauma you have been through, the more difficulties you are likely to attract.

Somehow, life continues to perpetuate painful and complicated circumstances. It can seem that the trouble and drama are never-ending, that there's no escape. It's as if we were programmed to suffer, a never-ending loop of misery... trapped forever.

Why does this happen? Why is it so difficult to break free from the past? Why do those negative patterns keep reappearing in our lives? The sad truth is that as long as the past remains unresolved, the problems are likely to keep appearing in your life.

Many of my clients in the first session, when I'm asking about their problems, say, *'I've done so much work on myself, but I'm still miserable, and bad things keep happening all the time. I'm jinxed... When is this going to end? I try and try, and nothing changes. It's too much now!'*

The problem here is that, although the client may have worked with resolving the past at a conscious level, it is still not fully released at the subconscious level. If it were, the client would not keep attracting negative events into their life.

So how do we know when the past is not resolved? It can be difficult to be objective and make a true assessment, but there are some indicators.

Tell-tale signs of being trapped in the past:

- Being triggered by specific events or circumstances

- Having anxiety, fear and panic attacks that appear randomly for no reason

- Feeling depressed and unable to get out of bed in the morning

- Being stuck in a negative state of mind or repetitive negative thought loops

- Feeling overwhelmed and out of control

- Being excessively tearful or emotional

- Feeling fearful

- Experiencing flashbacks of traumatic memories

- Experiencing confusion or 'cloudy' or 'muddy' thinking. Not being able to think clearly

- Finding it difficult to focus and concentrate

- Having difficulty making decisions

- And of course, attracting the same negative stuff over and over again

It is important to note that with life's pressures, we all feel this way from time to time. But if these feelings are persistent and overwhelming, or you wake up with negative feelings every morning or have that messy *'muddy clouded'* mind where you can't think straight, then there is more work to be done.

When I was still in the grips of trauma, I woke every morning, feeling heavy and depressed, like a big black cloud was pressing down on me. I would drag myself out of bed and go to work, on automatic like a zombie, because I had no choice. I had responsibilities.

Arriving at work and starting the day, it wasn't long before my negative patterns appeared. At exactly 9 am every morning, depression transformed into anger. Anger at my parents for the pain and trauma they had caused, the mess they had made, and subsequently, the mess I had made. It was all their fault!

My biggest desire was to have them in front of me right now, so I could tell them exactly what I thought… let them know how much they hurt me and what terrible parents they had been, and how many problems I had in my life now, because of them.

All day my mind would loop through my trauma and pain, the loss and devastation, over and over and over again, like a broken record. By the time I dropped into bed at night I was mentally and emotionally exhausted! But I'd toss and turn all night long, unable to fall asleep, and wake the next morning feeling depressed all over again, with the anger starting again at exactly 9 am.

This was my pattern. Every. Single. Day. And night.

Looking back now, I can clearly see why my life was a mess... and it wasn't because of what my parents had or hadn't done. It was because I could not let go of the past. I was filled with resentment and self-pity, endlessly rehashing the past and keeping it alive with my anger.

Many of us fall into this trap, and it's understandable. But wearing your trauma like a tattoo burned into your skin is not good for you or your peace of mind.

So, if you find yourself stuck in a similar pattern, overwhelmed by negative emotions and stuck in a loop of destructive thoughts, like a broken record, you are definitely not done with the past. And sadly, neither is the past done with you.

So, the first thing to do to take back control of your life is to understand trauma: what it is, and how it affects us. So, let's break it down.

Emotional triggers – What they are, and why you feel so out of control

Triggers originate in the subconscious mind. The subconscious mind is exactly like a computer...

It does all the things a computer does:

- It collects 'data' / information

- Records the information – your subconscious mind has recorded and stored every moment of your entire life!

- Processes that information

- Draws conclusions based on the information collected

This is its job, and it does its job well, to create a vast database of knowledge for us to be able to understand life and the world in which we live.

Also, at the top of its list of functions is the task of protecting us and keeping us happy. And part of the role of keeping us happy is to protect us emotionally. And the way it does that is to remind us of past trauma and problems. It keeps these memories fresh in our minds to warn us of pitfalls, mistakes, and emotional pain, to help us *avoid* these situations in future. It's as if it plants a red flag in the middle of that trauma so that we will never forget it.

The problem is that all this focus on our problems means that we can't let go of the past. To make matters worse, the subconscious mind does not understand the concept of time, so every time it brings up a negative memory to try to warn us to *'be careful,'* we feel as if that trauma is happening again right now, at this moment. The result is that the trauma becomes compounded... it adds layer upon layer of trauma.

Let's say this person was 3 at the age of the first trauma:

Age 3 – First trauma – creates the 1st layer of trauma

Age 7 – Second trauma or triggering event – becomes 2 layers of trauma

Age 10 – Third trauma or triggering event – becomes 3 layers of trauma

Age 15 – Fourth trauma or triggering event – becomes 4 layers of trauma

Age 23 – Fifth trauma or triggering event – becomes 5 layers of trauma

Each time another trauma happens, it amplifies the original trauma, and creates an additional *'trauma layer'*. Not only that but, because the subconscious mind does not understand the difference between what is real and what is imagined, ***each time the person is triggered, the mind reacts as if it were another real trauma and adds another layer too.***

So, as time progresses, more and more layers are added, and the trauma is intensified and becomes more deeply embedded in the mind.

As if that weren't complicated enough, along with the progressive layers of trauma, comes a very interesting phenomenon. The fact that the subconscious mind does not understand the concept of time, means each time you are triggered, *in that moment* it takes you back in time to the *emotional age of the very first trauma.*

Many clients tell me something curious, '*I don't understand it. The trauma happened years ago, but my anxiety is getting worse and worse. I'm not a child anymore. Why is this happening? Everything frightens me now.*'

So why would the client's anxiety get worse, not better over time? Because every time the client is triggered, *in that moment*, she feels as helpless as that 3-year-old. So, the mind adds yet another fearful experience to the data bank… So, the trauma state grows and grows.

So, when there is unresolved trauma, and this person is triggered:

At 7 years old – in that moment, emotionally they react and feel as if they are 3 years old

At 10 years old – in that moment, emotionally acts and feels like a 3-year-old

At 15 years old – in that moment, emotionally acts and feels like a 3-year-old

At 23 years old – in that moment, emotionally acts and feels like a 3-year-old

And even now, at the age of 32 – in that moment, emotionally acts and feels like a 3-year-old

So, at that moment, when this person is triggered, they revert to the emotional age of the very first trauma. This explains why it is so difficult to think clearly when you are being triggered!

A three-year-old experiencing trauma:

- has zero problem-solving abilities

- is easily overwhelmed

- feels really frightened

- can't think straight

- doesn't know how to begin to solve such an adult problem

Seeing it like this helps your mind to make sense of the way you feel when you are triggered. You might feel helpless, tearful, overwhelmed, fearful, angry, or any combination of these or other negative emotions… exactly the way a three-year-old might feel in a bad situation.

One thing to bear in mind is that it is *only during an emotional trigger*, that we feel helpless, like that three-year-old. The rest of the time we could quite possibly function as normal adult human beings.

In some people, the difference between who they are in normal life and who they are when triggered is as vast as day and night, and some people are completely dumbfounded by their own reactions.

I sometimes hear things like, *'I'm a confident woman, I run my own company, and have a lot of responsibility. But when a trigger hits, I feel completely out of control. I can't think straight and have to run to my office to calm myself.'*

So, everyone reacts to and handles their trauma differently. I also think that pretty much everyone has experienced trauma in some form or another, and we all have the emotional scars to prove it. And emotional scars tend to create a fear of the same thing happening again.

And while all this is very interesting, it still doesn't solve the riddle of why the past keeps repeating itself, why we keep attracting the same patterns we strive so helplessly to avoid. Surely, one might think, that if the subconscious mind is trying to protect us, it would not keep attracting the same patterns and trauma into our lives... Right?

No. Wrong. And I'm going to explain exactly why.

Why does our past create our future?

Well, here's the thing: protecting us is only one of the jobs the subconscious mind does for us. It has another very important job. Like a computer, it's also a processor. It processes information in order to make sense of it and understand it. It needs to understand what happened and more importantly, why.

And to understand any situation, the subconscious will focus on the past, and more importantly will physically recreate past difficulties, so that it can *'study'* them. Part of its job is to analyse and understand the world as you experience it. And it will keep recreating that particular situation until it does understand.

So, if the past is not resolved, you could find yourself experiencing the same challenges, attracting the same situations, and facing the same problems, over and over and over again, endlessly.

And I can tell you all about repeating patterns showing up in life because for many years I was tormented by ongoing trauma and drama. I was a drama magnet! It followed me everywhere I went and seeped into every area of my life, no matter how much I tried to avoid it.

And I blamed it on my trauma. If I'd had a good childhood, my life would be different. I would be happy, and confident, and I would have the perfect partner, the perfect job and the perfect life. Instead, my life was, for the most part, an unhappy miserable mess.

There was one area of my life where I was doing well - work and career. When I started working, I discovered, much to my surprise, that I was smart, driven, focused and ambitious. In my very first job, I was soon promoted to training new employees due to my attention to detail. It wasn't long before I set my sights on climbing the corporate ladder. Promotion followed promotion, and it felt great.

But it wasn't all sunshine and roses. Even here, in my workplace, trauma and drama crept in. In one particular job, things went horribly wrong through no fault of mine. I was subjected to attack based on language discrimination, of all things!

I was frustrated and angry about all the drama that kept appearing in my life... I wanted serenity and peace! I craved tranquillity and a drama-free *'normal'* life, like everyone else. I'd had enough drama to last me a lifetime!

But it followed me everywhere. It tracked me, and it manifested itself in every single facet of my life as if it were attached to me like a limpet mine, just waiting to explode. My life was filled with drama and problems, and I lived in fear of what would happen next.

In one particular job, I became aware that my very conservative, repressed and narrow-minded boss, who

FROM TRAUMA TO ABUNDANCE

constantly picked on me and humiliated me, was using my laptop after hours to secretly view pornography! I was horrified and nauseated.

I had to find another job! I started to focus on manifesting the new job, pushing it hard, forcing it to happen, willing it to happen. It took me six months, but I did it. I got a great job with a prestigious company, lots of perks, a fantastic salary, and, to top it all, it was really close to home. I was thrilled.

This was the first time I had experienced a positive result with manifesting. Forcing it and willing it to happen had yielded results, which I found really interesting, given my complete failure to manifest anything at all previously.

But it was exhausting and draining, as I focused all my attention and energy on willing the new job to come my way. And now it had worked.

But there was a problem: My intense focus had yielded results, yes, but ultimately, not the kind of results I was looking for. It didn't take me long to realize that this job, which was my last paid employment before I opened my own business, was riddled with – yes, you guessed it – more drama!

Office politics, the secretary sleeping with the boss, jealousy, bitchiness and backstabbing, lies and dishonesty. Drama, drama, all the way!

Always the drama. I was angry and frustrated, But I was also puzzled about the same old patterns re-emerging everywhere I went.

I had a question: How was it that, no matter how hard I tried to create peace, The Universe kept sending me drama?

I had been true to my promise to myself to spend two years alone, so there were no upsetting and messy relationships. But The Universe seemed determined to make up for it in other areas of my life... such as work.

I felt hunted as if there was a target on my back. And I felt oh soo sorry for myself! Why wasn't I allowed some normality in my life? I felt helpless and trapped. I was so angry at life and spent my days ranting furiously in my mind, at my parents, at The Universe, at The World, and at everything and everyone. I was desperately unhappy.

I thought about changing my job again, manifesting a new job... But with a deep feeling of inner dread, I knew it was pointless. I had tried and failed.

I was trapped.

The human mind – Why does the past keep repeating in our lives?
There are several factors at play here:

- The mind *recreates experiences* in order to *'study' them* and *'understand'*, to *make sense of life*

- Negative emotions *are transmitted as powerful and intense waves*

- The mind assesses your past, labels it as *'reality'* and *'reproduces'* and *'recreates'* it

So, let's look at these in more detail:

The mind recreates experiences in order to 'study' them and 'understand', to make sense of life:

The human mind is a fascinating thing. It quite literally is a problem-solving computer. There is the conscious mind, which is the logical part of the mind; the analyst, the mental processor.

Then there is the subconscious mind, which stores information about you. It's the database of information about who you are, what you like and don't like, your personality traits, and what life is about for you. This is also where our programming comes from. How we react to life is automatic and is defined by our subconscious mind.

Together, these two parts of our minds are constantly analysing what life is and how we react to it so that we can understand ourselves and understand life. The truth is that one of the main purposes of life is to understand it.

When a negative event happens and upsets us, our emotional response indicates to the mind that we don't understand what just happened. And this is true. Have you noticed how stunned and confused you feel when something terrible has just happened? There might be other emotions as well, such as fear, anger, or sadness… But we always feel stunned and confused.

You might find yourself saying, *'How could this happen? I don't understand…'*

It is very normal to feel this way and to say these things, and of course, you don't understand. And neither does your mind. And the more shock and horror, the stronger your reaction, the more likely you are to develop an issue with that particular set of circumstances.

Now understand that the mind is a problem-solving computer, so it recognises the shock in your reaction, and it also recognises the fact that you can't comprehend what just happened. So, it labels the event as an *'unsolved problem'*.

The problem is that the mind does not like unsolved problems because its job is to solve problems, to find answers, to comprehend and understand life. And when you react in shock and can't understand what just happened, it marks the event as *'something in need of study'*.

So how does it handle this need to study the incident, to understand it? ***It recreates the same event.*** And it will continue to recreate *'the problem'* over and over, again and again until it has fully understood and found *'the solution'*.

Negative emotions are transmitted as powerful and intense waves

The second part of the difficulty stems from the mind being a transmitter... very much like a radio transmitter. It sends out signals. So, when an upsetting or traumatic event happens, and we have a strong reaction, these intense negative emotions are transmitted outwards in powerful waves. And what you send out, is exactly what you get back. The exact replica of the distress signal you *'transmit'*, or *'send out'*, will most definitely return to you, in one way or another.

The mind assesses your past, labels it as *'reality'* and *'reproduces'* and *'recreates'* it

The third part of the problem is that the mind takes a snapshot of the past and superimposes it on the future.

And every time you experience the pattern, it reaffirms, *'This is what life is. This is reality. This is what your life is.'*

And with each subsequent reappearance of the pattern, the belief becomes more deeply embedded into our mind as *'evidence'* and *'proof'*. And the more deeply rooted the belief becomes, the more it defines our *'reality'* until it is completely accepted by the mind. This then becomes your *'belief system'*, about yourself, your life and the world.

Our mind quite literally makes an assumption that based on past experiences, the future is likely to look the same. You need to understand that all the while the subconscious mind is collecting data, it does this to form a picture of what *'reality'* looks like. This is why everyone's *'reality'* is different.

The subconscious mind quite literally thinks, *'XYZ happened in the past and that is proof that XZY will happen in the future too.'*

So, why do bad things keep happening?

Three things are going on here:

- If something bad happens and you react in disbelief, your mind will recreate the event until you do understand it

- The mind is a transmitter and negative emotions such as shock and horror get transmitted outwards in powerful waves which actually attract the negative event back into your life. What you send out, is what you get back. And the more intense the emotion, the more likely the event is to reappear

- The mind takes a snapshot of the past and assesses it as *'Reality'* and *'My Life'*, and *'The World'*. It then integrates and accepts this *'reality'* as *'real'*, and sets about recreating this *'reality'* in your future

You see, it's very simple: as long as you hold on to the past, with all its intense negativity, you're actively creating the identical blueprint for your future. That's why, when I manifested my new job from a place of desperation, The Universe sent me a job with just as many problems.

This is one of the reasons it is not a good idea to manifest from a state of desperation. Yes, you will attract something, but that something might not be the thing you were looking for, and it will likely bring even more problems into your life.

So how do you want your future to look? Look around you now… What have you created in your life? Is your life ruled by misery? Do you keep attracting the same situations? Do you struggle to break free from the past?

The good news is that the future is not written in stone… It's not a done deal. I was wrong when I thought there was no escape, and that I was trapped.

You *can change your life*, and I'm going to teach you how so that you can heal the past and break the spell of doom and gloom, just the way I did!

CHAPTER FIVE

Heal The Past

What You Are Holding Onto, Is Holding You Back!

Overcome Trauma, Drama, Unhappiness and Unfulfilled Yearnings

We all have *'stuff'*. People who have hurt us, disappointments in life, upsetting and traumatising events... in short, the *'bad stuff'* that has happened to us. But holding onto your stuff is a lot like holding onto a lump of hot coal. The longer you hold on to it, the more it burns. And if you think about that hot coal, whose hand is it burning? Yours. Holding onto stuff hurts you - not the person who wronged you. It's that simple.

I heard something once and it really put things into perspective for me: *'Anger is something you give yourself for someone else's bad behaviour.'*

This really drives the point home. Why would you continue to hurt and upset yourself by holding on to stuff, when the other person has most likely either moved on, forgotten about the incident, or is simply not prepared to take responsibility?

But letting go is not as simple as it sounds. How do we let go when someone has wronged us or traumatised us? One of the most powerful ways of moving on is to start observing and acknowledging your patterns, thoughts and feelings, objectively and without judgement.

When I started to observe my patterns, I became aware of how angry I was. I spent hours daily in abject misery, admonishing my parents for all their wrongs. I felt hopeless, drowning in misery and unhappiness. I couldn't see the wood for the trees and felt overwhelmed by life, with no clue of how to begin solving my problems.

I'd been for therapy… a lot of therapy! It hadn't helped much at all. They kept asking how I felt, but I was blocked and traumatised, and couldn't talk about the emotions which overwhelmed me. I'd also developed a deep distrust of people, so I found it difficult to open up.

I'd read self-help books, and they helped to some degree. But I was still very stuck in my misery.

But one day, while shouting at my parents (in my head), I suddenly had a thought… and it was a different thought than I had ever had before, and it took me totally by surprise.

And it went something like this: '*Sharon, you do realise that you are speaking to dead people, right? Your father is gone, your stepmother is gone, your stepfather is gone… Newsflash… dead people don't talk!'*

And suddenly I understood something which had previously completely alluded me: I was never going to get that apology. Dead people can't apologise.

The simplicity of this thought stunned me… I had never thought of it that way before. And the logic was unassailable. I was never going to get that apology!

In an instant, I saw myself from the outside… how I had continued to punish myself for years and years. How I had held on to the pain and anguish and allowed it to taint my world by refusing to let go of something that was long dead.

Almost instantly another thought came. *'Yes, it is true… my childhood was destroyed because of the trauma. I didn't really have a childhood. But why would I continue to allow the trauma to destroy my adult life as well? Why give it another moment of my precious time? This is my life and I choose to be happy from now on… In fact, I'm going to have my childhood now!'*

And just like that, I let it go. I surrendered. And along with surrender came acceptance and peace of mind. I felt as if I'd just put down a huge burden as if a huge weight had just been lifted.

It felt so good to just let it go! I felt free and light, and I could breathe! I suddenly realised I'd been holding my breath for what felt like forever!

My mind went quiet... It was a beautiful feeling. All the inner turmoil, the confusion, the anger, the messy thoughts, the blaming, the resentment... all vanished in a second. And with that, came peace of mind.

And the patterns of drama and trouble which had haunted me for so long began to magically dissolve and melt away.

Just like that – the pattern was broken.

Noticing your patterns is the first step to healing. You need to observe them without judgement, and without blaming.

Acceptance is definitely the second step.

It's good to note here that acceptance doesn't mean accepting that what happened was wrong. It means accepting that it happened, so you can move on. It also means accepting that whoever did you wrong is unlikely to apologise, if they haven't done so already.

It means setting yourself free from carrying the burden of the trauma.

When we have been hurt, anger and pain can cloud our judgement. We want to be heard. We want that apology. We feel it will validate us and release the pain and trauma.

And society is full of cliches, like, '*You need that apology so you can have closure*'.

The truth is that even if you do get that apology, it's probably going to feel flat and empty because it can't even begin to make up for the emotional pain and turmoil you have already suffered.

And as for closure, here's the truth: *there is no such thing as closure!* Accept this truth and you will set yourself free. It's as simple as that.

Just let it go. *There is no such thing as closure!*

Once you have accepted this, that nothing can make it right, nothing can fix it, and nothing can change what happened, then you can move on.

One of my favourite sayings is, '*The past has passed... away... Gone forever. And thank goodness for that!*'

What happened, happened, but it's over. Isn't that a beautiful thing to think about? You are free, and you have the rest of your life ahead of you. Don't allow the past to rob you of your future! Just let it go.

This is your life, and you have a right to be free, to be happy and to be abundant. So let that stuff go.

Here's another nugget of truth: That stuff, the bad thing that happened, was not your fault. It was not your fault. It was never your fault!

Please repeat this out loud to yourself: '*It was not my fault.*' It helps! This especially helps if you were a victim, such as during childhood trauma. Children often blame themselves and feel terribly guilty. I know I did. So, say it a lot, until it really sinks in! *'It was not my fault.'*

And even if the problem was with you, and you made a mistake, as long as you learned something from the experience, it has value, and you can move on. So let go of that guilt. Negative emotions serve no purpose. Stop carrying that stuff around!

One last thought here: other people make mistakes too. We are all human and humans are flawed… we all make mistakes. I sometimes think that society, with expectations of perfection, is a real pain in the a**

We are led to believe that *'other people'* had *'perfect childhoods'*; that a *'mother'* is someone who is nurturing and kind and bakes cookies, gives hugs and cuddles and never raises her voice. A *'father'* is someone strong and confident, who believes in you, praises you and reads bedtime stories.

I have news for you. These stereotypes don't exist! We are all beautifully flawed human beings. So, remove those labels, and let go of those expectations, and you will be a lot happier!

Another thing to remember is that everyone, including our parents, our spouses and our friends and family, in fact, all of us, are the product of our own troubled past. We are all rowing together in the same boat, doing the best we can. Sometimes we fail. Sometimes we mess up. It's all part of life.

Life is messy and beautiful and interesting, and hopefully we learn something along the way.

So, drop your expectations for perfection... perfection in others, and perfection from yourself, and you will be a lot happier. And when you are happy, you are abundant. So, choose to be happy, if for no other reason than you want to be abundant!

It sometimes helps to have empathy for other people's problems. Even if your parents messed up badly, it helps to remember that they probably went through bad stuff too.

One of my most beautiful thoughts of forgiveness has been, *'How would anyone know how to be a good parent, if they didn't have good parents?'*

I love this thought, and it really helped me to heal and move on. I hope it does the same for you.

Notice your negative patterns and habits, those little tell-tale signs of your inner emotions

When I first started working with the Law Of Attraction, I made a point of examining all my habits to understand why I was not able to manifest good things in my life. One of the things I noticed was that at night I slept with my hands in tight fists as if I was ready to fight the world or defend myself and punch anyone who stepped on my toes. And that was exactly how I felt about life at the time. I had been dealt so many blows, that I trusted no one and nothing. The world was a *big bad place*, and I was not going to allow anyone to push me around anymore.

What I didn't realise was that the more I fought with the world, the more the world fought with me! I was literally creating my own misery by being stuck in the past. Because what you are holding onto, is holding you back!

And I repeat: *what you are holding onto, is holding you back!* It's that simple.

And there I was, quite literally holding onto my stuff, by sleeping with closed fists at night. So, I made a choice to start sleeping with open hands. When I went to sleep, I would make sure my hands were open.

And as I drifted off to sleep, I would think, *'I am safe and protected… I am open to abundance… Good things are coming my way…'*

If I woke during the night, and I found my hands in fists, I would open them as I drifted back to sleep. First thing in the morning, if my fists were closed, I would open them. It took some effort, but slowly, the old habit of sleeping with tight fists lessened, and finally disappeared completely, as I began to sleep with my hands open to abundance.

It's about noticing those odd habits, those outdated ways of thinking; paying attention to the little things, such as your body posture… Do you slump your shoulders, or drag your feet? Straighten your posture, pull your shoulders back, push out your chest, and lift your feet... Notice your patterns and make a dedicated decision to change them. First, you notice the pattern, then you set about changing it. And you keep training yourself until the new pattern is firmly in place. It's the little changes that make the biggest impact.

And of course, the good news about the past is that it has passed. It's over!

The Past has passed

The nature of the past is that it has passed, and it's never coming back! The door to the past is closed. Not only is it closed, but it's locked! It is never coming back. So, it is safe now to leave it behind, lock the door and move on. The sooner you let go, the sooner you can create the life of your dreams.

One of the things that I love about the past is that it's over. All the bad experiences are over. It's done and dusted, very much like the water that flows under a bridge... That particular water only flows under that particular bridge once. Once that water has passed, it's passed. Gone forever.

And as you read these words, maybe you can feel yourself putting the past into the past, where it belongs... And moving on... And creating a better future for yourself.

And I wonder if you can feel that sense of relief, that whatever happened is done, and that it's gone forever, or whether you are just really looking forward to a better future, a brighter future, knowing that the worst is over and that the best is yet to come…

Have you ever considered that having a traumatic past might have given you some amazing gifts?

Of course, having been through trauma makes things a little more challenging, but it's not all bad news. Did you know that your trauma, your problems, and the difficulties you have been through, may well have given you some amazing gifts? Gifts that have automatically set you up to go far in life, and to be extremely successful…

Not sure if you believe me? Read on to discover more!

Overcoming The Past

So, let's switch this around a little bit… Can you allow your mind to ponder the fact that maybe, just maybe, the difficulties, the problems, the pain, and even the trauma, may actually have set you up for huge success in your life? Does that sound crazy or what?!

But consider this: what if your obstacles, your problems, in fact, your entire history has given you tools… tools that you can apply to great benefit in your life today… Tools you can use to boost yourself when the going gets tough… Tools you can use to reach undreamed-of potential… Tools that you could not have learned in any other way.

I've always been a thinker, and my 21st birthday was a big milestone in my life. I found myself evaluating my life, who I am, why am I here, and what is my purpose in life… But like a lot of 21-year-olds, I didn't have a clue how to answer these big life questions!

But it started me thinking and reading.

Self-help books seemed a good place to start, and I stumbled onto a technique used by many successful people: modelling yourself on someone you admire. The best way to model yourself, I discovered, is to read autobiographies of famous and successful people, to see how they did it. At the time I was looking for that one common denominator, that magic pill which had catapulted them into such great success. And that one common denominator, when I found it, was one of the most interesting discoveries in my life!

I soon discovered that the life stories of these successful people all had one thing in common: these people all came from exceptionally difficult circumstances. Every last one of them. From traumatic childhoods to abuse, tragedy and difficulties in life.

At first, I was astounded… how did all these people who came from such tragic circumstances make the transition to such huge success? It just didn't make sense! Was there a link or was it just a coincidence? And if there was a link, what was it and what did it mean?

As I analysed this curious phenomenon, I came to an amazing realisation: it wasn't that they transcended their problems to somehow achieve success, but rather the opposite: that their adverse circumstances had actually primed them for success!

This led me to another question: what is it about going through difficulties that sets someone up for achievement and success? Exactly how does that work?

And as I delved deeper into this puzzle, I began to understand. You see, when someone goes through extreme circumstances, such as trauma, they are quite literally pushed to their limits. They are forced to dig deep to cope and overcome whatever crisis they are going through.

Often these incredible survivors of trauma and abuse go through the tough times all alone, with no support whatsoever, so they are forced to draw strength and resilience from within themselves.

This exercise of continually being pushed to the limit, having to be constantly alert to explosive situations, always in survival mode, teaches that person very specific skills... extremely useful skills that can later be applied to achieving great goals.

Not only does trauma teach us incredible skills, but this way of thinking, of finding solutions, of being our own inner strength and support, becomes a habit, a very specific and permanent way of thinking in life.

Of course, everyone is different, and we all experience different traumas and difficulties, but whatever you have been through, it has equipped you with some very powerful tools and skills.

For example, I once did a course on face profiling just for fun. Face profiling is the study of how facial features are related to personality. My teacher looked at me and said, *'Determination is one of your strongest points. You never let anything stop you. I can see from your chin that you never give up!'*

I just laughed, but it is completely true! I never give up! I absolutely will persevere until I achieve my goal. I don't know how to give up! I must admit that it's one of the things I really like about myself.

If I fail at something, I might be upset for an hour or two, but then I start to bounce back. I re-examine the problem… to find a different way to make it work… or to understand it.

And I know that I got this trait from having been emotionally knocked down so much in life. I taught myself to bounce back quickly. When I was little, I had no one to lean on, no one to support me, and no one to *'prop me up.'* I learned to do that for myself. I had to be resourceful. I had no choice. Now I love the strength and resilience this has given me.

No matter what problems and setbacks you have experienced in life, and we have all experienced at least some setbacks, they have taught you skills. They have equipped you with strengths and talents.

I wonder which of these skills and characteristics you might recognise in yourself:

- Thinking out of the box (lateral thinking)

- Determination to succeed

- Resourcefulness

- Intuition... *'knowing things'* or having a *'gut feel'* or a *'sixth sense'*

- Possessing exceptional problem-solving abilities

- Thinking on your feet

- Quick to respond

- Absolute calmness in the face of a challenge or disaster

- Being an excellent judge of character

- Able to make snap decisions wisely and confidently in a split second

- Bouncing back from setbacks really quickly

- Creativity and inventiveness

- Spotting opportunities that others may have missed

- Possessing unshakable belief in your abilities

- Being driven to have control over your life and fortune

- Being able to stay focused on a goal

- Drawing strength from within

- Having a greater understanding of life

- Taking responsibility for your own happiness

- Taking the initiative to make things happen

- Empathy... a deep understanding of people and their problems

- Inspiring others

- Having a sense of humour and not taking things too seriously

These are invaluable life skills, and they cannot be taught, and they cannot be bought. They can only be acquired, through hardship, through being pushed to our limits... by walking through the fire and going through the most gruelling challenges in life.

I like to think of tough times and trauma, as *'brain-gym'* or *'boot camp for brains'*. Going through immense difficulties quite literally alters the way your brain works! It rewires your brain and teaches you skills; skills which, once you recognise them, you can use to achieve ANYTHING you desire.

How does it feel to realise that as a victor of trauma, you are:

- More resilient

- More likely to succeed

- More likely to be able to get the best out of life

And… best of all… it means that you are far more likely to be able to manifest easily!

Doesn't that change how you feel about yourself and what you have been through?

Understand now, that your trauma has not limited you. Instead, it has equipped you with all the skills you need to create the best life for yourself!

I fully believe that we were born to overcome our blocks and difficulties. We are meant to find solutions and benefit from all that *'brain gym'*, all that hard training.

And that feeling you get when you start to recognise your potential and overcome the obstacles is so empowering and so beautiful. It feels as if you're truly alive. Every cell, every molecule, every atom tingles and vibrates with pure joy and anticipation of the future!

You were born to succeed! This is your birthright. And everything you have been through in life has equipped you with the beautiful powerful tools, to make this happen for you.

When you see things from this perspective, it all becomes worthwhile. It starts to make sense. You can start to make sense of your life.

Obstacles are merely a rite of passage, a teaching technique to train your brain's powerful skills so that you can become your very best self! So, start noticing and practising the tools and skills you have been given, to build yourself a wonderful life!

It's a bit like studying for a degree, finally passing the exam, and feeling both a sense of relief and a sense of great excitement for the future.

The Past is a G I F T

G - Great

I - Insights

F - From

T - Trauma

Your trauma has given you gifts and strength

The truth is that obstacles have been placed on your path for you to overcome and transcend them. It makes you strong, gives you resilience and teaches you wisdom and empathy for others. These are all amazing character traits to help you to become amazing!

And you need to be amazing to push the boundaries. See how far you can go; how much you can achieve. You were born to do this. It's your birthright to free yourself from the past, it is your birthright to succeed and be happy and prosperous! You have earned it, and now you get to claim the prize!

Once you understand that the things you once saw as limitations are actually stepping-stones, powerful gifts in disguise, you will begin to understand that trauma, limitation, disappointment, disadvantage, and even failure, can become the very foundation for your hugely successful life.

Do you realise how hard you worked to acquire these skills? Can you give yourself the credit now and allow yourself to claim your reward for all that hard work? Let's face it, it was not easy! But you have earned the right to be at the top, to claim your place, to experience success, and to live a joyful and fulfilling life, rich with abundance.

And isn't it amazing to think about that now?!

EXERCISES FOR THIS CHAPTER

- Do you have emotional triggers and patterns?

- What are they?

- How do they make you feel?

- Do you know where they come from?

- What negative patterns do you have?

- How do you sleep at night? Curled into a protective ball? Tight fists?

- Which skills do you have from having been through tough times?

- What makes you special and different?

- How can you use these skills and gifts in your life?

- Can you give yourself permission to start utilising these amazing skills to start succeeding in life?

- How does it feel to have these resources?

- Can you give yourself credit for having done so well in the face of great difficulties?

- Can you finally, actually start believing in yourself now?

CHAPTER SIX

Heal The Now

Handling Difficulties In Life With Ease

You might ask what is Healing The Now about? This is all about learning how to take control of this moment right here right now. It's about feeling calm, no matter the situation. It's about transforming negativity into positivity and coping with ease when things do go wrong. You can only truly start to have success with manifesting when you are in control of your mind, body and emotions. And to be in control, you need to function in the world from a place of inner peace and learn to create powerful and unshakable states of happiness, no matter what is going on in your life.

The reward is that you start to feel good about the World, and the World starts to feel good about you too. The result is that you naturally start attracting great things. You can literally watch your world transform in front of your eyes! And when that happens, manifesting wonderful things for yourself comes easily.

But being in control of our own mind is a tricky business. How do you stop reacting to bad situations, when everything goes wrong, and life is difficult and stressful, or you are hurt, targeted, bullied, sabotaged, abused, or abandoned? How do you even begin to feel good about life, when life treats you so badly?

In Chapter Five, we spoke about acceptance and empathy. These are powerful tools, but they are by no means the only tools available to overcome the past or to Heal The Now.

In this chapter, I share some wonderful resources and insights into starting to solve your present-day problems, taking control of your emotions, and feeling better about yourself and life.

Recognising the problems

When we look at our present day-to-day problems, it's important to realise that we actually created these problems. Our mind is programmed to solve problems. Take that idea one step further and you might begin to understand that your mind will keep creating the same problem over and over again, in an effort to solve the problem.

It's almost as if our mind sees the problem, recognises the pattern, and tries to resolve it, but can't find the solution. So, it reactivates the problem to appear in your life again, so it can examine the problem again. It literally won't stop recreating the problem until it finds the answer or resolves the problem.

How do you know when the subconscious mind is doing this? Well, a good indicator would be that you find yourself manifesting negative things, or attracting drama and problems, or the same hurtful scenarios keep reappearing. This indicates that LONA, or The Law Of Negative Attraction, is active in your life.

How do we fix these problems?

We have been taught that to solve a problem, we need to focus on it and *think it through* so we can process the available information, and *sort things out* and *fix it*. And of course, this has huge value, but we can easily get in the way of our own mind and become overwhelmed. It almost seems that the bigger the problem, the less clearly we can think about it.

That's because, in an effort to solve the problem, we are operating from the conscious mind, and can easily become trapped in compulsive thoughts, worry, anxiety, and fear. And the fear and anxiety, in turn, trigger old feelings and patterns of self-doubt and insecurity. The result is that we feel overwhelmed and even less capable of making decisions.

To add to all of that, daily stresses, work deadlines, too many tasks, not enough time, bills to pay, kids to fetch from school, and supervising homework, all add to feelings of not being able to think clearly and an inability to cope.

With all this going on, it's easy to come to the conclusion that there's something wrong with you because everyone else seems to cope so well with their lives. So, you find yourself thinking that you are **not good enough.**

You can see how easy it is to find yourself drawn into focusing on your faults and being pulled into a negative downward spiral. This is because you have lost clarity and can no longer be objective.

And when we are feeling stressed, exhausted, or strung out, and stretched beyond what it seems we can endure or accomplish, our thinking becomes clouded and we find ourselves going round and round in circles, and somehow, instead of starting to feel better, we feel progressively worse, as though we were being sucked into a spiral.

And the deeper we get, the less clearly we can think, the more anxious we feel, and the more we worry and stress. The result is a feeling of being completely overwhelmed, which drags us down still further and seems to somehow confirm just how useless we are!

The real truth is, that all this stress, worry, self-blame, and negativity actually blocks the subconscious mind from helping us find the solution. We are bombarding the subconscious with so many demands and problems simultaneously, that it doesn't know what to tackle first. So the subconscious mind simply throws its hands in the air and says, *'I don't know!'*

The result is a feeling of being completely overwhelmed, a deep feeling of inadequacy and self-blaming and guilt for not coping.

So what's the solution?

How do we overcome this obstacle of feeling overwhelmed, so our mind can start to solve the problems?

You start by calming your mind. The calmer you can be, the more clearly you can think, and the quicker the solutions come. And I know how difficult it can be to try to think calmly when you are in a stressful situation! It's a catch-22. We need to be able to think clearly and calmly, but we can't because we are worried, stressed, anxious, fearful and overwhelmed.

This is where you really need to give yourself a break. You are not superwoman or superman! Stop expecting so much from yourself all the time! You are a human being with normal human feelings. And simply admit that right here right now you are feeling overwhelmed.

Step One – Become aware of your emotions – Naming it

One of the most powerful exercises is to become aware of your feelings and to put a label on your emotions. So, you can just say out loud: *'I'm feeling overwhelmed.'*

Giving it a name and labelling it already starts to calm the mind because it begins to answer the question *'What is wrong with me?'* And what is wrong is that you are feeling overwhelmed. And everybody feels overwhelmed from time to time. This is a very normal reaction to stressful and upsetting situations.

So go ahead and tell yourself *'It's okay to feel overwhelmed/sad/stressed… This is not a new feeling. I've been through this before. And this feeling has a beginning… a middle… and an end…'*

This really helps to define the feeling with simple logic. When you add logic into the equation, it helps the subconscious mind to understand what is going on and why.

Be aware, though, of how you say this … Don't say *'I **am** overwhelmed'* but rather *'I **feel** overwhelmed...'*

There's a big difference in this phrasing. In the first example, you are **labelling yourself as being overwhelmed**, you are claiming the emotion and making it part of you. But the truth is that you are temporarily **going through** something. You're experiencing the emotion.

Remember, if you label yourself, with the phrase, *'I am XYZ'*, this becomes a limiting belief. So be careful not to unnecessarily label yourself negatively.

In the second phrase, *'I feel overwhelmed'*, you are acknowledging that this is a feeling that you are going through at the moment. Do you see the difference?

Step Two – Allow the emotion and embrace it

Once you have named the emotion, the next step is to stop fighting it, and just allow it to be…

One of the best ways to allow an emotion is to sit in front of a mirror and look at your face. Examine your face, your eyes, your mouth, and your expression, without judgment…

Understand that you are allowed to have reactions and feelings. Give yourself permission to feel this emotion. Feelings are a human reaction to emotional pain, and you are human.

And as you examine your face, notice the expression… Don't try to change it. Just let it be.

Then, again, say out loud to your image in the mirror, *'I'm feeling anxious / overwhelmed/frightened…'* Or whatever emotion you are feeling, such as anger, frustration etc.

And say this out loud three times.

Now take a long slow deep breath in through your nose, all the way into your stomach, then a long slow long sigh out, through your mouth.

Do this three times.

Now check in with your emotions again. Notice the calmness, the relief.

Negative emotions are the subconscious mind's way of letting you know that you are not coping well. It's like an alarm clock going off and trying to wake you up. If you ignore the alarm, it will continue to ring. The same with a negative emotion. The more you resist or suppress it, the more persistent it becomes.

Once you surrender, acknowledge and embrace the emotion, it will release, and you will start to feel calmer and more at ease with life.

We think that we need to hold on so tightly to our emotions to '*control*' them and that if we let go, we might collapse. In reality, the opposite is true. Trying to resist or control a negative emotion takes a huge amount of energy and effort. It drains us and leaves us feeling exhausted and broken.

When you let go of the need to suppress and resist a negative emotion, the need to control it falls away too. The result is that the negative emotion itself will dissipate, dissolve, and melt away.

Negative emotions can only be sustained if you are feeding them with resistance in an attempt to suppress them. Once you have surrendered to the emotion, your mind will start to feel calmer.

So, stop fighting the emotion. Just allow it to be.

Step Three – Distract your mind – live in the moment

After acknowledging, embracing, and letting go, this is a good time to distract yourself. Re-centre yourself, make yourself a cup of calming camomile tea.

Empty your mind, stand in a patch of sunlight and focus on how the sunlight feels on your skin, go for a short walk, get a breath of fresh air, or if it's cold, turn on the heater and warm your hands, focus on the sensations of the flow of heat on your skin. Or if it's hot, switch on the fan or aircon. Focus on how that feels.

The more you focus on simple things, the more you are bringing yourself back to this moment and connecting to inner peace and tranquillity.

This is also a good time to practice another technique I love: slowing time down. I know this may sound crazy, but believe me, I've been working with this technique for over 10 years in my practice, and it is one of the most effective and powerful ways to take control of your emotions.

If you think about it, when we are angry, upset, anxious, or worried, something very interesting happens to time... it speeds up. Your thoughts start racing, your breathing comes shallow and fast, your heart starts to pound, and everything starts to blur and spiral out of control. It's like a spring winding up, getting tighter and tighter and tighter!

When this happens: Just. Stop.

For one split second. Just. Stop.

Take a deep slow lazy breath. And slow time down. Imagine a clock winding backwards, going slower and slower and slower. Your thoughts start to slow down, your mind becomes quiet, your breathing returns to normal, your heartbeat slows, and you start to feel more in control.

It helps to focus on your breathing. Breathe in slowly through your nose, and then exhale a long slow sigh through your mouth. Empty your lungs completely, and then another deep breath through your nose, slowly.

And so, in this moment, right here, right now, all you need to do, is breathe... Slowly... And deeply...

And as your breath slows down... Your thoughts slow down... And time slows down... And everything slows down...

The slower you go, the more you slow time down. And the more you slow time down, the calmer you become, as you start to feel more and more in control.

Other ways to calm the mind and learn to live in the moment are exercise, yoga and meditation. These techniques teach you how to discipline your mind and connect to a state of inner peace and tranquillity. These are powerful ways to feel better about yourself and life.

Step Four – Be the observer of your patterns and how you react to them

Which patterns keep appearing in your life? How do you react, and which emotions come up for you? Which other problems also triggered this response in you? Sometimes you can even find the root of the problem... where it started.

Quite often the problems go back further than our conscious memory. Write down all the times and all the instances you can remember which are connected to these patterns. Go back as far as you can. Then ask your mind with a sense of curiosity, *'Where did this start?'*

It is important to detach from the emotions when you are digging for the root.

I had an interesting experience where my memory unexpectedly took me back to the root of a problem, which occurred when I was eight months old! I had always wondered why I didn't much like dogs. The strange thing is that I love animals... all animals. But not dogs. The mere thought of a dog made me cringe in revulsion. I especially didn't like them licking me. It was a completely involuntary reaction over which I seemed to have no control.

For a long time, I just accepted this part of myself. It wasn't a fear of dogs... I just didn't like them. At all. And of course, every time I visited someone with a dog, the dog would make a beeline for me. It was awkward. I would hold my hands up to avoid being licked. I wished the dogs would go to someone else! But every time I went anywhere there were dogs, they would run directly to me.

Looking back, I can see that it was one of my patterns.

But on one particular day, while relaxing in the sunshine, my mind wandered over this strange reaction I had to dogs. I could not remember ever having been attacked or hurt by a dog, and in any case, I wasn't at all afraid of dogs. Just this strange reaction... That involuntary shiver of revulsion... It was odd.

'Where did this come from?' I wondered curiously. Instantly an image flashed into my mind. I was just eight months old and sitting flat on the wooden floor in my grandmother's flat. The sun streamed through the window and reflected off the shiny polished wood flooring.

Being only eight months old, I had recently learned to sit up alone, without support from my mother. I can still feel how proud I felt because my little body could actually balance... I was still very wobbly and tipped over easily.

My grandmother had a dog. A little dog with very sharp claws. And it kept jumping up against me, its claws digging into my arms. I had a vision of myself trying to pull away. It was jumping against my right arm.

My grandmother kept calling the dog off me. I didn't like the dog and its sharp little claw on my arms... it hurt. But that wasn't the issue.

The whole thing came to a head when my grandmother stepped out of the room. The moment she was gone, the dog dashed towards me. As I recoiled to lean away, I lost my balance and toppled over.

As I lay helplessly on the floor screaming, the dog ran to my face and started licking me inside my mouth. I can still feel how helpless and horrified I was. I could not get back up, so I was just lying there helplessly, with the dog licking inside my mouth, and me screaming.

Of course, my grandmother ran back in and got the dog off me, but the damage was done. From that day, I disliked and distrusted dogs intensely.

And yes, I do love dogs too now, because I love all animals. And I no longer shiver in revulsion every time I see a dog. But I would never own a dog. It just wouldn't be fair.

So, start asking yourself questions: '*Where did this come from?*' The answer might not come immediately, but you will have posed an interesting question to your mind. And the mind loves questions. And it will look for the answer.

Write the question on a piece of paper and put it under your pillow… Allow your mind to linger on the problem as you drift off to sleep.

It is really important to detach yourself from the intensity of the problem. Try to be impartial and curious about the root of the problem. The more intense or negative the emotion, the less likely it is to surface. A casually curious mind is a great way to find the root.

I was lucky enough to have a spontaneous regression, just by sitting in the sun and allowing my mind free reign to go to the root of my strange reaction to dogs. It is possible that you too could uncover more information, just by allowing your mind to go back over time. I think that the reason I remembered it is because my memory was jolted by the fact that I was sitting in the sun, just the way I had been, when the incident happened, all those years ago.

If you're lucky, you could also discover more about the roots of your problems, or at least some other connected incidents, which might be relevant. And if your mind doesn't provide you with the answer, there is always hypnosis. Hypnosis is amazing for finding the roots of all sorts of problems, no matter how far back they go!

At the end of the day, it might not even be necessary to remember the roots. But you do need to learn how to handle the emotions.

So here are the steps:

1. Name the emotion

2. Allow it to be

3. Embrace it

4. Distract your mind

5. Live in the moment

6. Slow time down

7. Observe the patterns

8. Get the understanding, the knowledge

You don't even have to do all of these. Use the ones which work best for you. These techniques of managing and acknowledging your emotions are powerful ways to take control of *The Now.*

And when you can take control of now, by becoming calm, by being in the moment, this is not only a great way to heal the past, but it's also a great way to heal the now; to contain and reduce and eventually eliminate triggers, negative emotions, fears, anxiety, blaming and anger.

This was one of the very first techniques I myself used to successfully let go of my anger and resentment when I first started succeeding with manifesting. You see, in order to manifest wonderful things, you need to master this moment, right here, right now, at least to some degree.

There are other techniques which are just as effective for managing problems, triggers and emotions, such as Cognitive Behavioural Therapy (CBT). This is a great tool for deactivating emotional triggers without needing to find the cause. With CBT the therapist will work with you to give you solid techniques to cope better and desensitise triggers and how you react to them.

You need to change your emotional reaction to triggers, to be more in control, and more at peace to manifest good things.

Step Five – Analyse: what are you learning that you could not have learned in any other way?

What are you learning from these situations that you could not have learned in any other way? This is important, this is the crux of the matter. Because you are here to learn so you don't have to keep repeating the lessons!

Also, analysing, questioning and observing without judgement will change your perspective about the problem. Not only does it become a learning experience where you get to know more about yourself, but you will also start seeing these difficulties as a set of circumstances that benefited you in some way. I spoke about this in Chapter Five – Overcoming The Past and the GIFT (Great Insights From Trauma) you received by going through that trauma.

Ways to take control of the present moment

- See steps 1 to 8 in the table above, from naming the emotion through to getting the understanding and the knowledge.

- Analyse – what are you learning that you could not have learned in any other way?

- Understand the GIFT you have got from the incident

The bottom line is that we need to make peace with the present moment. Only from a place of (relative) inner peace can we be in control of our destiny. Of course, no one is perfect but to be able to cope just that little bit better, you need to understand yourself, so that you are not on an emotional roller-coaster all the time.

All this learning and understanding is, of course, the ultimate goal. Because once you learned the lessons and understood what they mean, how they affect you, and what you have learned from experiencing these difficulties, you have power over your own mind, body and emotions.

And isn't that awesome and empowering?!

And self-mastery of the mind, being in control of your mind, body and emotions, is the cornerstone of all greatness – including manifesting your own best life!

Chapter Seven

"Good Will"

Helping others without expectation of anything in return has been proven to lead to increased happiness and satisfaction in life.

I would love to give you the chance to experience that same feeling during your reading or listening experience today...

All it takes is a few moments of your time to answer one simple question:

Would you make a difference in the life of someone you've never met—without spending any money or seeking recognition for your good will?

If so, I have a small request for you.

If you've found value in your reading or listening experience today, I humbly ask that you take a brief moment right now to leave an honest review of this book. It won't cost you anything but 30 seconds of your time—just a few seconds to share your thoughts with others.

Your voice can go a long way in helping someone else find the same inspiration and knowledge that you have.

Are you familiar with leaving a review for an Audible, Kindle, or e-reader book? If so, it's simple:

If you're on **Audible**: just hit the three dots in the top right of your device, click rate & review, then leave a few sentences about the book along with your star rating.

If you're reading on **Kindle** or an e-reader, simply scroll to the last page of the book and swipe up—the review should prompt from there.

If you're on a **Paperback** or any other physical format of this book, you can find the book page on Amazon (or wherever you bought this) and leave your review right there.

CHAPTER EIGHT

Getting Out Of Your Own Way

Break Away From Fear

Negative emotions block abundance, and all negative emotions stem from only one base emotion – FEAR

Looking at the heading of this paragraph, I can almost see your eyebrows raised in surprise. Could this be true? Is fear really the single base emotion of all negative emotions?

Surprisingly, the answer is a resounding yes!

So let's take a look at some negative emotions to examine this theory.

FROM TRAUMA TO ABUNDANCE

Anger is fear in disguise

Anger is one of the most common but also most destructive emotions, and one which causes huge blocks to manifesting good things for yourself.

But we all get angry sometimes, right? After all, it's human nature to get angry when things go wrong. Yes, that is true. But anger can become an automatic response to life, almost like a bad habit. A bad habit that not only blocks abundance but actually recreates and attracts the very problems that make you angry in the first place.

So let's take a closer look at anger, what it does to you, and what happens when you lose your temper (and, in the process, request *a large order* from The Universe, of *more things to make you angry)*.

The nature of anger and what follows when you get angry

Have you ever noticed that when things start to go wrong, and you respond with an outburst of anger, suddenly everything starts to go wrong! It's as if The Universe is saying, *'Oh, so you want to be angry? Well, here is more stuff to be angry about…'*

Remember, when you transmit a high frequency of any emotion, be it positive or negative, you can be sure that The Universe will fulfil the order you placed. And so, it responds to anger, by *'sending'* more problems so that you can experience more anger.

When we respond with anger, we are indicating that we do not accept whatever caused us to be angry. So what we are really saying is we don't understand the situation that caused us such anger. And we all know by now, that when the subconscious mind does not understand something, it will recreate the identical situation to *'study it'*.

The real answer lies in taking a moment to *decide how to respond*, instead of just exploding. Just breathe, and slow time down, using the methods I spoke about in Chapter Six. This will give you time to analyse the situation impartially. Become the observer of the situation, of yourself, of your emotions and the way you respond to certain stressful situations. Then, and only then, choose how to react.

This changes the energy of the situation completely. We are here on Earth to learn. So analyze, and learn, so you don't have to keep making the same mistakes, and learning the same painful lessons over and over again.

Even if the lesson is only, *why do I react with such anger?* And *where is this anger coming from?* Analyzing the situation as a whole, brings a deeper understanding. And deeper understanding brings clarity. And clarity resolves the need to become angry.

Also if you analyse the reason for your anger, you may realise that it came from someone who hurt or traumatised you in some way. And anger is a normal response to that trauma. But it is also a way to protect yourself from further harm.

For example:

- *'If I am an angry person, people will fear me and they won't harm me again.'*

- *'Anger makes me feel bold when I am frightened by a situation.'*

- *'Anger validates my pain – it proves that I am worth something.'*

- *'Being angry makes me feel alive – it proves that I exist.'*

But the truth is that whatever your reason for anger, it is based on FEAR. Fear of a past hurt or trauma repeating itself. So you use anger to try to control the situation. But the truth of it is, that when you lose your temper, you are doing the opposite – you lose.

When you lose your temper, you lose.

The best-case scenario is that you might win that heated argument momentarily, but the damage caused both to your own self-esteem and the relationship, is simply not worth it.

You see, when you lose your temper and get angry – you lose:

1. You lose control

2. You lose dignity

3. You lose the respect of others

4. You lose self-respect

You lose. It's that simple. When you lose your temper, you lose. And I don't know about you, but I hate to lose!

You could fool yourself into thinking that anger gives you control, but deep down, expressing negative emotions, such as anger, makes you feel unhappy and desperate. It's a losing battle, which drains your energy and sucks the joy out of life.

If you lose your temper, you lose! End... Of... Story.

But if you start to work with analysing the real reason for your anger, you will start to understand that all anger is actually rooted in FEAR.

And the moment you acknowledge that you are feeling fearful, and take responsibility for that fear, you can start to heal. Do the exercise of the mirror and repeating it three times. This will help to release the negative charge of the fear. Or invest in learning some anger management skills, or see a counsellor. You can even punch a cushion to release the energy, and if you can do this until the tears come, even better. Tears are healing, and a beautiful way to let go of negative emotions.

But find a way to deal with the anger, so you can be free of the debilitating negativity it causes.

Another block to manifesting is Self-Sabotage.

And yet, self-sabotage is just another form of fear. So let's take a closer look at Self-Sabotage.

Self-Sabotage comes in many forms:

- Holding yourself back from opportunities

- Making bad decisions

- Procrastination

- Negative thinking

- Laziness

- An *'I don't care' / 'I'm not worth it...'* attitude

- Alcohol or substance abuse

Let's take a quick look at the root of these problems:

Holding yourself back from opportunities can be based on low self-esteem, a lack of belief in your abilities, and fear that things could go wrong or that you wouldn't cope. There could be a feeling of stuckness, of knowing deep inside that you can do it, but being too afraid to take action. The root cause here is FEAR. And when fear rules us, we can easily find ourselves too afraid to take on challenges. We would rather stay stuck and suffer in silence.

But if you think about it, isn't staying stuck much more uncomfortable and frightening than actually taking on that challenge? Holding yourself back is painful and makes you feel afraid and insecure. This is not a happy feeling, and neither is it a safe feeling, so staying in the *'comfort zone'* is anything but comfortable. The truth is, that holding yourself back creates yet more fear, which results in holding yourself back even more. Believe me, it is actually less scary to take on the challenge than to hold yourself back.

So you have a choice:

- You can stay stuck in the misery and heartbreak of self-sabotage

- Or you can face your fears and go for it

Why not see how far you can go and how much you can achieve? And notice how vital and alive you feel when you are stepping out of your comfort zone. So, say yes to a challenge today!

Making bad decisions is a common form of self-sabotage.

Here are some reasons people make bad decisions:

- You think you don't deserve good things

- Your parents set a bad example so *'that's the way things are'*

- You make decisions in haste and don't take the time to think things through

- You are focused only on yourself eg: overspending on your credit card

- You are focused on immediate gratification eg: too much partying during the week when you have work the next day

There are, of course, many other types of bad decisions, but whichever form the bad decision takes, it remains a bad decision. And the problem with making bad decisions is that this way of interacting with the world can become a bad habit, something we do without even thinking, as we muddle from one disastrous decision to the next.

A lot of times, people who habitually make bad decisions have low self-esteem, or think really negative thoughts, such as: *'My life is a mess... I'm a mess. I do stupid things all the time. It's who I am...'*

All this negativity is rooted in FEAR: fear of life being a mess, fear of being hurt, fear of turning out like your parents, and then finding yourself repeating their mistakes. Sometimes I think our biggest fear is the fear of disappointment. The feeling here is, *'I'd rather expect the worst than be disappointed again.'* This form of negative thinking can easily lead to making a bad decision, or holding back from something wonderful, out of fear.

One common and very destructive subconscious motivation goes like this: *'I might as well have fun now and pay the price later…*' But the price is a steep one as one bad decision leads to another.

But the bottom line is that every bad decision is rooted in FEAR.

So start becoming conscious of your decisions. Observe your patterns. Become aware of your thought processes. Slow time down before making a decision. Think things through. Take your time. Then consciously make a good choice.

This one action will change your life, believe me. I used to make terrible decisions all the time, and my life was chaotic. Until I made a conscious choice to start making good decisions.

So start making good decisions today. It will change your life too.

Procrastination is pretty much the same thing as holding yourself back – avoiding doing something because you fear failure, think you will make a fool of yourself, or fear the outcome.

But procrastination can also be rooted in putting things off because we feel lazy, or are avoiding facing something unpleasant. Procrastination can even be rooted in fear of success! Whatever the reason behind it, procrastination is absolutely FEAR-based.

The simple answer is to just do it! Get it done! You will feel amazing when it's behind you.

But it's not always easy to take action.

So, here is a simple technique for motivating yourself, and it goes something like this:

1. Think of a goal or something you need to do

2. Think about doing a kind of *'countdown'* from one to five

3. Tell yourself that when you get to five, you *will take action*

4. Start counting from one to five, and with each number, you feel more motivated, more enthusiasm and energy building up, getting stronger with each number you count

5. One, two, three, four, five...

6. And go!

It's amazing how well this technique works. This is a good way to start working with programming your mind, to get it to do what you want it to do.

Working with your mind is part of self-mastery. Becoming the master of your own mind is empowering and rewarding, and programming your mind brings inner peace and self-respect. These are great attributes and make you feel good about yourself. So put in the effort, start practising and working with your mind today. It's worth it. You are worth it!

The simple answer is to just do it! Get it done! You will feel amazing when it's behind you.

Negative thinking is FEAR in disguise. We all know negative people and the heavy energy they carry with them, and we might even try to avoid them because being around them sucks the energy out of us. You might even be negative yourself and notice the painful fact that people seem to avoid you

The fact of the matter is that negative thinking is a *fear-based habit*. This is usually brought about by previously having experienced pain and disappointment. And we think that if we expect the worst, we won't be disappointed or hurt again.

'If I expect bad things, I will be prepared. It won't hurt, and I won't be disappointed.'

Here's a wake-up call – negative thinking actually attracts more of that heavy oppressive stuff into your life. Remember LONA? The Law Of Negative Attraction?

If you expect bad things to happen, The Universe thinks you are placing an order for more problems and difficulties! Are you sure you want more problems, more things going wrong in your life? Is that what you really want? And how do you feel when you realise that you are actually attracting more negativity? Fearful? Yes, well I'm not surprised! Because negative thinking is definitely FEAR-based.

So change the way you think! It's time to let go of this fear of things going wrong, so it can let go of you!

You can take control of your emotions by living in the moment. This is a powerful way to overcome negative and fearful thoughts. I also like to observe my thoughts and when a negative thought pops up, I imagine it's a weed in the garden of my mind, and I pull it out and throw it away. This is another way of becoming the master of your mind. Notice the negative thoughts, uproot them, and throw them away.

The subconscious mind might be difficult to communicate with and might resist change, but imagination is a powerful tool to take control of your own mind. Invent your own ways of dealing with negative thoughts... shrink it with an imaginary magic wand, put it in a hot air balloon and watch it float away, throw it into the sea, or blow it up with dynamite. You can have fun with this, and just changing the energy to one of fun, already shifts those sneaky negative thoughts.

One thing I'd like to mention is that from time to time, we do get disappointed, and we do get hurt. There is no escaping it. But how you handle these challenges makes all the difference. Sometimes things go wrong, that's part of life! So accept that. And when things do go wrong, observe the patterns and watch your reactions; learn, understand and then let it go.

Laziness is a perfect excuse to get out of doing something that challenges us. To put it bluntly, laziness is an excuse to avoid participating in life... it's a cop-out. There is an attitude of: *'Couldn't be bothered'*, AKA, *'I don't care...'* Or, to be brutally honest here, *'I don't care enough about myself to put in the effort... I'm not worth it...'*

It's so much *'safer'* to not care, isn't it? To not be bothered. Rather not try at all, than to try and fail, right? No! Wrong!

People tell themselves they feel *'stuck'* and *'unmotivated'*. All this to hide from the real problem – FEAR.

The truth is you are not stuck, you're just not living. You're treading water, and getting nowhere. But we human beings actually crave making progress. It's the nature of being human. And when we are not making progress, we are only half alive. And that is not a comfortable feeling at all!

So you have a choice... Either you take action and face your challenges, and end up learning all sorts of amazing things about yourself, or you stay stuck in misery and laziness.

Are you really happy to be stuck, lazy and to cower in fear? Is that enough for you? I don't think so – if it were, you wouldn't be reading this book.

So, get involved with your life, deal with your problems, and start caring about you. Start putting in the effort. Start living!

The bottom line is that laziness and an attitude of not caring is based in FEAR. Fear of failure, fear of success, fear of disappointment, or fear that the result won't be worth the effort. This last excuse is totally null and void – it is always worth the effort even if you don't succeed because you learn, and when you learn, you make progress. And we humans were born to make progress. It feels right!

Of course, some people are genuinely lazy. But even then you have a choice – you can either be lazy, and suffer the discontent and disappointment in yourself, or you can put in the effort and start living. The choice is yours!

Alcohol and/or substance abuse is escapism. It's an effort to run away from, and escape our problems. Of course, many of us all do go through a *'partying stage'* of life, and that is not only okay but good for our self-growth. But a few years of partying and exploring who we are is not what I am talking about here. I'm talking about a lifestyle of substance abuse, be it alcohol or drugs, where this becomes a permanent way of life.

But using a substance to try to outrun your problems is a pointless exercise. Firstly, it is impossible to outrun or escape your problems. It's just not possible. And secondly, abusing substances brings its own set of heartbreaking problems, and creates yet more difficulties.

So why do people try to run from their problems? Because facing their problems brings up FEAR. It's that simple.

Summary of Self-Sabotage:

From the above examples, we can see how fear can affect our deepest motivations, block us, and prevent us from moving forward. It's a sneaky little thing that can creep into the deepest recesses of our mind and whisper all sorts of bad advice and suggest avoidance tactics, which cause debilitating problems in our life.

But the bottom line is, that self-sabotage is FEAR in disguise. And when we pull off the disguise, what we see is that there is only one problem. FEAR.

So let's get right down to it, and talk about FEAR

Fear is super interesting. The fear of something is often far worse than the actual thing we feared in the first place. Our imagination can easily run wild and create a scenario far worse than reality. Often the thing we fear so much never even happens. The problem is that logically we know and understand these facts, but it doesn't seem to help in the least to calm that deep feeling of dread that something awful might happen.

The reason it's so difficult to calm our minds is that fear is directly linked to our subconscious mind, and the subconscious is programmed to keep us safe. And it takes that job very seriously. It uses fear to warn us of possible danger, of approaching disaster, and of things going wrong. The fact that your subconscious mind keeps you safe and warns you of danger, would surely mean that it's your best friend, right? Not so much.

I had a client who came to see me – I'll call her Sally. *'I have a full-blown phobia of rats,'* she told me, shifting nervously in her seat, *'Even if I see a rat in a movie, I scream and run from the room… I can't even handle a picture of one!'*

She went on to explain that she once saw a rat at a waterfront shopping centre. *'I decided right there that I would never go to that place again.'*

Next, she saw a rat in a supermarket. *'That's it,'* she decided, *'I'm never going into another shopping mall.'*

As luck would have it, she next saw a rat in the street. It's interesting to note that we attract the things we focus on, positive or negative, so I was not in the least surprised that she kept manifesting rats wherever she went.

After she saw the rat in the street, she made another decision: *'I'm never leaving home again,'* she told herself, *'That will keep me safe.'*

Of course, it didn't. One day, in her back garden, what did she see? A rat.

'You won't believe what I did,' she told me, *'I jumped over a half-door into the kitchen, to get away from it.'*

My eyes widened. This was a middle-aged, unfit, short, overweight and very round woman. How on earth did she manage to jump over a half-door? But my mind already knew the answer to this riddle – her muscles had been fueled by adrenaline. I will talk more about anxiety and adrenaline in a later chapter.

'The worst of it,' She went on to explain, *'is that now I am afraid of everything. I used to love socialising with friends, but I started avoiding that, so now I have social anxiety as well. It took all my courage to come here today.'*

Her mind had quite literally imprisoned her by over-exaggerating the danger and suggesting a retreat from *'dangerous places'* in an effort to *'protect'* her. The result was that her world had shrunk and become a nightmare of unnamed dangers which lurked around every corner.

'I'm going crazy!' She told me tearfully. *'I can't live like this.'*

It was an interesting case. Apparently, her mother also had a fear of rats. This did not surprise me at all. We learn behaviours, including fears and triggers, from our parents. In psychology, this is called modelling. More about this in a later chapter.

But I knew there had to be more than an inherited fear for a phobia of this magnitude. In the next session, we did some regression. She went back to being six years old. They were very poor and their house had holes in the floorboards, and of course, rats came up through those holes.

One day, little six-year-old Sally was sitting on her mom's bed while mom got dressed. As Mom put her foot into her shoe, there was a rat inside. Mom lost the plot, and Sally was also extremely traumatised watching Mom's terrified screams.

Once we found the root of her phobia, it was easy to work with it to release her fear of rats, so that she could get back to living a normal life.

But you can see from this story, how the subconscious mind can sabotage our peace of mind with suggestions to avoid things we fear.

'If you avoid this situation,' Our subconscious is quick to suggest, *'you will be safe.'*

This couldn't be further from the truth. The truth is that the more you avoid the situation, the more power it has over you. And the more power it has over you, the more your fear grows. And of course, the more fearful you are, the more fearful things you will automatically attract into your life.

The bottom line is, that when we fear something and try to escape or avoid it, the negative energy, that pure raw fear, is transmitted outwards in powerful waves. Naturally, The Universe responds to these powerful waves by sending you more of whatever it is you fear so that your mind can study it and understand it; so you can solve the riddle of fear and why it controls you.

The best way to overcome a fear is to face it and embrace it. Don't allow fear to rule your world. A little bit of fear is a healthy thing, of course, so I'm not saying you should throw caution to the winds. But overwhelming fear that controls your life and your decisions is not healthy on any level.

So, you have a choice – either you continue to allow fear to rule your life, and accept that The Universe will continue to manifest situations which will trigger and frighten you, or you find a way to resolve your fears. And the best way to resolve a fear is to face up to it and acknowledge it. Admitting fear does not make you weak – it makes you strong.

So if you are feeling fearful, embrace it. Acknowledge it.

In Chapter Six, I mention a technique for managing feeling overwhelmed and anxious, by looking in the mirror and repeating the emotion three times. The same technique works beautifully for acknowledging fear.

'I feel fearful and frightened... fearful and frightened... fearful and frightened...'

You see, the more you avoid a negative emotion, the more power you give it over you. Once you surrender, acknowledge, and embrace the emotion, you are releasing it. And when you release it, you can start to feel calm and at ease with life.

There are some excellent therapies for resolving deep-seated fears:

- Hypnotherapy

- Cognitive Behavior Therapy (CBT)

- Acceptance and Commitment Therapy (ACT)

So, we have learned a lot in this chapter about the emotion of fear. But there is one more very important lesson to learn:

Did you know that there are only two base emotions on planet Earth? Love... and..? Guess what the other emotion is? Most people answer, Love and Hate. Being polar opposites of each other, that would make sense, right? But that is not true. Because the base emotion that causes hate is FEAR!

Hate is not a base emotion. Fear is.

So, the two base emotions in the World are Love and Fear. Everything comes down to that.

And if you are living in fear, get help. Heal yourself. Because you deserve to be Living in Love. And when you are living in love, yes, you guessed it, it is easy to manifest wonderful things.

So start manifesting from a place of love, and watch your world transform in front of your eyes!

CHAPTER NINE

Learn To Love You And Like You

Be Your Own Best Friend!

Loving yourself is a much-misunderstood concept. I think that society has given us a very distorted view of what it means to love yourself. Society likes to label things and loving yourself has been given a bad rap.

When we hear someone say, *'Doesn't she just love herself!'*, or *'He sure does love himself, doesn't he?'* This is not a compliment... It is a judgement that means someone is considered to be vain, arrogant and self-centred.

I have a vivid memory of this exact topic coming up on the sports grounds at school when I was a teenager. At the time, I was in boarding school, in my first year, so I was still a newbie and wet behind the ears, eager to fit in and be accepted. One day, while walking on the field with a group of girls, one of the girls in my group, Alice, pointed to another girl walking across the field.

'Doesn't she love herself!' Alice commented, her voice dripping with sarcasm.

The girl being pointed to was doing nothing special… She was just walking across the field. But she was a top athlete who was always winning awards for sports and was, somehow, also a top scholar. A real superstar.

At the time I did not understand the jealousy and insecurity that had fuelled Alice's comment. What I did understand very clearly was that it was dangerous to stand out and be exceptional.

Instantly I felt myself shrink down and close up. I desperately wanted to be accepted, and the risk of being seen as someone who loved herself was far scarier than shutting down a part of myself to be accepted.

I can clearly remember thinking that *'loving yourself is not okay – it's a bad thing'*. And I definitely didn't want people to say that about me! So, I made myself small and insignificant.

Looking back, I want to hug that younger version of me and say to her, *'No, you've got it wrong.'* I want to tell her to be brave, to be herself, with all the wonder and beauty and messiness that being yourself means. The teenage me was so lost, but so brave! Looking back, I can see that it was all part of her learning. And I wouldn't change a thing!

So, yes, society loves to label things. And truly, there's nothing wrong with that... We label things so that we can process the information about that object or situation, so we can understand it and know what to expect from it.

But I believe we sometimes go a little overboard with the labels. We've become so obsessed with labelling everything that we can hardly breathe for the fear of creating a label for ourselves. We care far too much about what other people think of us. And that filters down as self-judgement, and, of course, fear. Loving yourself carries a stigma. It's a label of conceit, vanity, and boastfulness. It's sad that self-love is such a deeply misunderstood concept.

But I'd like to expand a little on the difference between loving yourself and being boastful and full of yourself. Noticing someone in the room who seems to be very confident, that confidence may not always be as real as it looks.

Confidence can be learned and is not always a true reflection of someone's self-worth. Always seeking to be the centre of attention, being the loudest person in the room could quite easily mean that this person needs validation from others to feel worthy... That this person could be coming from a place of insecurity, and that they don't much love or like themselves at all

And sometimes the louder people are, the more unsure they are about themselves on the inside. I'd like to note here that loudness is not always a sign of insecurity... sometimes people are naturally loud, or they genuinely are very confident. But sometimes it's a sign of insecurity. And insecurity is not love, it is FEAR. So here we are, right back to fear.

Remember... all negative emotions stem from fear, and this is a classic example of exactly that.

So loving yourself is not loud and boastful. Loving yourself is a gentle, nurturing inner feeling of support and unconditional acceptance and approval of self. Loving yourself is the ability to believe in yourself, support yourself and be able to put yourself first, draw firm but gentle boundaries, stand your ground, and feel zero need to defend yourself when attacked, because you don't need to. You know who you are, and you like and love who you are, and that is solid.

The beauty of it is that once you get to the point of truly loving yourself, you never forget it. Once you get it, you get it. And the funny thing is that when you get it, it seems profoundly simple, and you will wonder why you didn't get it before.

But how many of us have this warm fuzzy feeling of genuine self-love? I think most of us have it, to some degree, but we really need to prioritise it in ourselves and turn it up. You need to feel good about yourself, support yourself and really care about yourself, to successfully create and attract the life of your dreams.

In my hypnosis practice, I have a questionnaire: the questions I ask my clients so that I can get to know them a little better, and the things that hold them back in life.

One of the questions I ask is a simple one, but it's something that many people battle to answer: *'What do you like about yourself?'*

The question is a revealing one. It helps me ascertain where someone is in their beliefs about themselves. Of course, it also helps me to see where the problems lie, and how deeply they run.

And the answers I get are always interesting. Some people say with an embarrassed laugh, *'I'd rather tell you what I don't like about myself...'* As if liking yourself were something to feel guilty about. This is because we've been taught that telling someone what we like about ourselves is 'bragging'. It goes against what we have been taught... It's *'bad manners.'*

Loving yourself actually starts with liking yourself. And of course, some people do get it right, when, in answer to this question, they smile and start listing the things they like about themselves, in a simple and non-dramatic way, as if this were the most natural thing in the world. And I love to witness this. It always stirs my heart, and inside I'm cheering them on. *'Yes, you've got it!'* It makes my heart smile.

But some people say flat out, *'I don't like myself.'* And this is really sad because here, it's not about holding back because it's bad manners to boast. It's about someone who dislikes who they are, at a deep level. And I can totally relate. When I was younger, I didn't like myself either. Often, the clients who say this are the ones who have been through a lot of trauma.

But I also know that somewhere inside them is that little voice we all have… The voice that refuses to be silenced by pain and abuse and trauma. And in these people, that little voice is saying something very different to what they are telling me.

That little voice is saying, loud and clear, *'I love you so much that I have brought you here today, to start healing. I believe in you, and I care for you, and I know you can do this. You deserve happiness.'*

And it is my job to reconnect them to that voice. The inner voice that cannot be stilled. The beauty of it is that we all have that little voice. The only thing you need to do is to learn to tune in, to listen to it.

We are actually all born with this voice. When we first come into this world, we are born loving ourselves. Babies and toddlers are filled with wonder at the world around them. Toes, fingers or glasses on someone's face are fascinating! You can see the curiosity and delight on their little faces.

So, what happened to that little one, so full of innocence and wonder? Life happened. And life can come with some very hard knocks and lessons. But one of the most important lessons I think we need to learn is how to love ourselves, despite being told we are unlovable, despite what other people have done to us, despite having gone through trauma and pain, and despite the deep disappointment of finding out that the world is not the wonderful place you once thought it might be when you were a baby staring in wide-eyed awe at everything around you. The lesson is to learn to love yourself the way that little baby loved themself.

In previous chapters, I have explained how your past creates your future. In fact, I would go one step further and say, not only does your past create your future, but *you create your world according to how much you value yourself...* This is really important so I'm going to repeat it:

You create your world according to how much you value yourself!

So, I want you to take a look around you right now and make an assessment. Ask yourself, '*What have I created?*'

And as you examine your life, your circumstances, the people in your life, and how these people treat you, it's an extremely accurate reflection of, not only your expectations about life but also how you feel about yourself. And while nothing is perfect, if there are deeply distressing circumstances in your life, or if you are stuck in an unbearable and painful situation, it means that you need to take a good honest look at how you feel about yourself.

You might not be keen to do this exercise of looking around and seeing what you have manifested, and it might come as quite a shock to you that you actually attracted these circumstances in the first place. But it is a wake-up call. The truth is that everything around you is a mirror image, not only of your beliefs but also of how much you care about yourself.

If your life is a mess, or there is ongoing trauma, or you are battling financially, then, yes, this is a reflection of your belief systems and upbringing, but it's also an extremely accurate barometer of how much you love and care about yourself.

This might be a bitter pill to swallow, but once you start taking responsibility for yourself, who you are, what your problems are, your relationships, your job/business, your finances, where you live, and the circumstances which surround you... Then and only then, can you start to fix it.

The day I took stock of my life for the first time, it was a shock to acknowledge what I had created. The mess, the drama, the abuse I attracted... The lack of money, problems at work, being bullied and targeted... The realisation that all these issues pivoted around one common denominator, me, was a huge shock. I saw clearly for the first time that I was in the middle of it all.

At the time I didn't realise how little I loved myself and how this was reflected in my life. But I clearly understood that I had somehow created everything around me. That realisation shook me to my core... It was like a light bulb flashed in my mind. It was one of the biggest 'AHA' moments of my life.

That was the day I finally stopped playing the blame game. That was the day I stopped feeling sorry for myself. That was the day I finally took stock and said, *'This is me... all of this is me. I created it; I attracted it into my life... It can only be me. I did this – to me!'*

And in that moment of crystal clarity, I finally understood it all. It was as if the world stood absolutely still for a moment in time. The silence in my mind was deafening as I took stock of the life I had created for myself.

We are so good at placing the blame on everything and everyone but ourselves. We tell the people around us, *'You don't make me happy.'* We absolve ourselves of responsibility and lay our happiness at the feet of others. *'Here,'* we say to the people in our life, *'This is yours. It is your job to make me happy.'*

The truth is that it is not anyone else's job to make you happy. It is your job. And we are very good at seeking happiness in all the wrong places. Shopping sprees to make us feel more important... Binge eating to comfort ourselves, but which actually does the opposite as we gain weight, lose control, feel worse about ourselves, and so eat more to comfort ourselves. It's a downward spiral of misery and self-loathing. We try to buy love from others by holding ourselves back, to make other people feel better about themselves.

But I think the worst of it is when we give away our power and expect others to *'make us happy.'* The job of creating your happiness starts with taking responsibility for your life and owning it.

But it can be difficult to love yourself and be happy when you've been dealt a bad hand.

'It was not my fault... I was a victim,' I can almost hear you saying. And I agree, it might not have been your fault, and maybe you were a victim. But you are no longer a victim. And even if you are still trapped by circumstances, there is always a way out. Find it. Reach out. Get help. Get out. Being a victim is a choice, so decide to make a different choice now.

And really, if you think about it for just a moment, being a victim is not much fun, is it? Being a victim sucks! Being a victim keeps you trapped in the past and trapped in misery and pain.

I know it's been hard. I know you have suffered. And I know it is difficult and scary to change. But remaining trapped in the past is much scarier. You are much stronger than you think, and you are ready to heal. Look at what you have already come through. Isn't it time, now, to move on, to face this, to get out, and to let this stuff go?

So, just for now, how would it be to do just that? To let it go... To be over it? Aren't you actually over it already? Aren't you bored with the misery? Aren't you bored with attracting more of the same mess, over and over and over again?

How would it be, to feel the lightness of putting down that heavy load you've been carrying for so long? Just... Let... It... Go.

Exercise:

Take in a deep breath through your nose, and as you breathe out through your mouth, just let it go – just blow it away... Let it go... It's over. It's done.

The truth is that the door to the past is already closed, and it's never opening again. In truth, the door to the past is not only, closed... it's locked!

Of the three tenses, Past, Present and Future, only two of them are alive: the Present Tense and the Future Tense. The past is dead; static; frozen. And it cannot harm you anymore.

So stop knocking on that locked door... The past no longer has any power over you. Walk away. Not in anger, but in love. Love for you. Respect for you. Caring and support for you. Nurturing you. Being there for you.

As previously mentioned, one of my favourite sayings is: '*The past has passed... Away... Gone forever...*' Isn't that an awesome thought? Isn't that something to celebrate? You're free to move on now.

And as you let go, even if it's just a little bit for now, and a little bit tomorrow, and a little bit the next day... Maybe you can allow yourself to imagine that your life is changing because of this one action. Imagine shaking off all that trauma, all those tears and all that pain... Just walk away.

And as you walk away and free yourself, your life will change, I can promise you that. You will start to feel lighter, more carefree... You will find yourself laughing more, having more fun, and starting to enjoy life. Doesn't that sound great? You are so ready for this – you know you are! You can change your life today.

I love the concept of time, and that a single moment can change everything. And could you imagine that this moment, right here, right now, is changing your life? A single thought can change your whole world! It did for me, and it can for you too.

The truth is, we all have choices. So, you can choose to change the thoughts you think, the words you speak, and the way you feel about yourself... And I urge you to make that choice today. Choose to change the way you think about You!

Let go of the stuff, take responsibility for what you have created, and take ownership of your own happiness. You are important. And putting yourself first means letting go of continuing to punish *yourself* for things that *other people* did to you in the past.

I think you are more than ready to let go of the blame game, to stop feeling like a victim, and to move on. Start changing how you feel about yourself, the world and your place in the world. You can choose your world. It's that simple.

So be courageous, look around you, take stock, see what you have manifested, and take responsibility. Taking responsibility is always the first step toward healing. And when you heal, your inner and outer world will automatically change too.

The role of guilt and how it stops us from loving and honouring ourselves

There is one last point I would like to mention here, and that is the role that guilt plays in our inability to love and accept ourselves. Guilt is a double-edged sword. It is linked not only to feeling bad for something we have done, but also to punishing ourselves for doing that thing. And we punish ourselves by blocking our own happiness, and by manifesting painful things. At the very least, the heavy negative energy of guilt will automatically block your ability to manifest good things for yourself.

As long as we continue to feel guilty, we are going to continue to punish ourselves.

And *self-punishment* can take many forms:

- Blocking abundance... Be it an abundance of joy, an abundance of money, career success, a loving and supportive partner

- Manifesting all sorts of problems and trouble for yourself

- Or any of the problems we spoke about in Chapter Seven, such as self-sabotage, making bad decisions etc.

There have been studies proving the link between ill-health stemming from emotions such as depression, negativity and fear, all of which can easily be traced back to feeling guilty. This just goes to show how deeply self-punishment can run, and how devastating it can be in our lives.

And along with guilt comes our dear friend, FEAR.

But what about when you *have done* something wrong?

Of course, guilt definitely creates fear: fear of being punished, fear of being exposed... And the burden of hiding what you've done can be debilitating. All this fear can be so strong that that in itself, can actually attract problems, and manifest havoc in our lives.

The gnawing feeling that *'I've done something wrong, and now I'm going to have to pay for it...'* is not a great feeling.

But it's more than that. You see, when we avoid owning up to something we have done, we lose faith and belief in ourselves... We no longer trust our decisions and actions. We no longer trust ourselves. And that, I think, is the bigger price to pay.

The truth is that hating yourself for what you have done, wallowing in negativity, toxicity, and poisoning your life serves no purpose. Conversely, punishing yourself does not make you feel better... It makes you feel worse! You cannot undo what is done. Guilt serves zero purpose.

So how do you fix your guilt and regrets when you've done something wrong?

You need to find constructive and positive ways to release the guilt so that you can move on. The first step is to own up to what you did... To take responsibility. *'I did something wrong... I feel guilty... I shouldn't have done that.'*

Next, take action – do one or more of these:

- Approach the person you wronged and apologise, face to face

- Write a letter or email to that person

- Do a private little ceremony... Write a letter apologising and admitting your wrongdoing, then burn it to release it

- If you are religious, say a prayer to ask for forgiveness or go to confession

Here are some other non-toxic ways of dealing with guilt:

- Do some community service

- Volunteer or donate to a good cause

- Do something nice for someone

- Pick up litter on the beach or in a park

When you do good, you feel good. And when you feel good, you can let go of the guilt.

Nobody has to even know what you are doing or why you are doing it, but do what you need to do to release it. Work that guilt out before it destroys your life! And when you take action and make amends, do these things consciously... Be aware that you are doing penance for your wrongs. That way, you will be able to release the guilt and set yourself free.

Feeling guilty without cause

The other side of the coin is someone who feels guilty about everything. This is not what I'm talking about here. If that is the problem, it might be that are being hard on yourself and don't feel good enough? So you need to ask yourself who made you feel that way? If you are not able to resolve this within yourself, it would be good to get some therapy and resolve these feelings.

Don't keep punishing yourself for something you didn't do; don't be hard on yourself and expect yourself to be perfect! We are all human and we all make mistakes. Life is not perfect and neither are we. Stop beating yourself up.

The truth is that perfection is an illusion. Learn to love and accept yourself, and stop feeling guilty about everything!

Ancestral Guilt

But guilt does not always come from something we have done wrong. It can also be *ancestral baggage*... That dark heavy stuff which has been passed on without question from generation to generation. This is a huge burden, both on us as individuals, and as a society, and it needs to change now.

I myself suffered from this generational guilt, which was passed on for no other reason than I was a child born into this family. And being a child, I had no way of defending myself, and no chance of saying, *'No thank you!'* In fact, as a child, I had no idea it was even happening. I only knew that by the age of 21, I felt guilty for being alive! And I hated myself and hated my life. Just the way all my ancestors had done in decades before me.

This ancestral baggage, this heavy weight, is done and over. We, this generation, are really lucky because we are living in the age of enlightenment and progress. Our ancestors didn't have access to the therapies and help available today. They didn't have the choices we do. So, it's time to deal with this and put that baggage behind us, once and for all.

It's time to create a different world. It's time to create light and joy and abundance in this beautiful world we live in. So please be aware, and don't pass on this baggage to your children. It's time to break those ties to the past and step into a better future.

And I believe this is already happening. I have seen the difference in this generation of parents, and how they encourage and love and support their children. Personally, I can't wait for this generation of kids to grow up and to see how they change the world. Because this generation of children has had help when needed, and have been encouraged to grow emotionally, speak up, and share their opinions. And it's beautiful!

When I look at my granddaughter, and the way that my daughter has brought her up, my heart overflows with joy! This 10-year-old is intelligent and funny, bubbly and joyful, alive and vibrant… When I was 10 years old, I was told to shut my mouth. But that's another story for another time. But it's quite funny because I always say, *'I wasn't allowed to speak as a child, and oh my goodness, I have a lot to say now!'* And I love that about myself, I really do. I love that I am outgoing and funny, empowered and brave and that I can speak up easily and confidently.

So let's build a new world. Let's encourage our children. Let's put down the baggage. Let's move on. Let's create a beautiful, vibrant, lively, abundant, nurturing and joyous world!

And it starts with our children. And it starts with you.

Learn to love yourself today!

CHAPTER TEN

Learn To Program Your Mind

Take Control of Your World

This is a beautiful part of your journey where you can truly start to feel more in control of your mind and emotions.

What are you programming into your mind today?

Let's start by taking a look at what information you are feeding your brain. On a daily basis, we are bombarded with information, entertainment, communication, music, advertising… It's a lot of noise with constant demands for our attention. And these demands play havoc with our senses, causing overload, stress, and negativity. They block our ability to feel calm and think clearly.

We are so out of touch with our thought patterns and belief systems, that we are hardly aware of how limited our thinking has become. No wonder we are battling with negativity, limiting thought patterns and blocked energy. The constant assault on our senses has limited our ability to think for ourselves.

In addition, there are many influences with very negative messages, such as violence and horror in movies, music with lyrics focusing on unfulfilled yearning, emotional pain and sorrow, negative people, and our habit of scrolling on our devices for (bad) news... The demand on our senses overloads our mind's ability to think clearly.

Remember, the mind is a transmitter, and transmitting a clear signal from a mind that is filled with noise, negativity and clutter is next to impossible. It's a bit like the old days when we were trying to tune into a radio or TV station, and all we could find was that awful hissing static, and high-pitched signals. When your mind is full of noise, all you are going to be sending out is a cacophony of static and unintelligible signals. So, it's not surprising that we manifest a mixed bag of stuff that we really don't want, which then stresses us out even more.

Our mind is a sacred garden, but we treat it like a dumping site. Then we wonder why we are not able to manifest beautiful things for ourselves. We need to be more aware of what we are feeding our minds.

Now I know this might seem a little far-fetched. How could it be possible that a movie or a song could have such an impact on our mind? But this is about more than just one movie or just one song. It's about constant negativity which assaults our brain with gloom, despair emotional agony and anxiety.

And yes, it's true, movies, series and songs are part of life. We look forward to switching off at the end of the day, and to being entertained, checking our social feeds, communicating with our friends and family on social media, and listening to the latest music. This is all very normal and a lot of fun. But it doesn't have to be the *only part* of life.

There is a strong need to balance the noise, stress and demands, with inner peace; to reconnect to a still-point of calmness and tranquillity. Finding the balance is key to feeling in control. We need to quiet our thoughts so we can send out crystal-clear signals to manifest our desires.

So, what can you do to find that inner peace and balance? To take more control of your mind and thought patterns? Quite a lot, actually!

The subconscious mind is a computer

Your subconscious mind, being an information processor, is constantly assessing and processing everything you hear, see, and experience. Every thought you have is monitored by this powerful processor.

And as more and more information comes in, the processor works faster and faster to absorb this new input. Then more information comes in and it speeds up even more. In an effort to keep up, your thoughts speed up, your breathing becomes shallow, and your heart can start racing.

Simultaneously trying to cope with the many demands of your everyday life, as well as this contestant input of information, can lead to anxiety, stress, and burnout. At this point, you might develop a headache and find that you can't think straight. It feels as if your brain is going to explode!

We've all experienced this feeling at some time in our lives. Even reading these words might cause your body to start experiencing some discomfort, as your mind recalls the awful feeling of spiralling out of control.

Exercise to calm the mind

So right here right now... Take a moment to just breathe... To go to a place of no-thought... Become aware of your breathing... The rhythm... How it feels... Notice your lungs slowly expanding with the in-breath... The soft sigh of your breath as you breathe out... And allow the out-breath to be longer than the in-breath... A nice, long, slow sigh breathing out...

Slowing time down

Imagine a clock... And the hands are unwinding... Anticlockwise... Slowly unwinding... Going slower... And slower...

And as time... Slows... Down... Your thoughts... Slow... Down... And your breath slows down... And your mind slows down... And you can start to tune into that quiet place in your mind. Notice how, in this space, there is no need for thoughts...

You might like to pick a spot to focus on... On the wall or in your garden, or even a picture on the wall... Anything is good... And allow your gaze to soften as you notice the details of this particular spot... Become aware of the inner quietness... Just for now.

And in this quiet space that you are creating in your mind right now... Allow yourself to focus on the temperature around you... Become aware of the surface you are sitting or lying on.... Consciously loosen your muscles. If your legs or arms are crossed, uncross them and allow them to fall loosely to your side... lose and floppy, like a ragdoll...

And your mind... becomes quieter still...

Take a deep slow breath in through your nose.... And out through your mouth... A long... Slow... Sigh... Letting go of stress and strain... And gently blow it away...

It's important to breathe in and out very slowly... You want to really slow time down.

So big... Slow... Deep... Breaths...

Remember, breathing fast will escalate anxiety and stress, so keep your breathing slow and rhythmic.

Do this a few times. It feels really good to put your full attention on your breathing for just a few moments…. Notice how your body responds… Loosens… And how your mind quiets down too… And your heart rate slows… And time slows down…

And in this moment, everything becomes quiet… In your mind… And in your body…

Now doesn't that feel good? Taking a few moments to just slow down your thoughts?

Of course, this might be easier for some people than others, but if you practice this slow breathing consistently, you will get results. Your mind will adjust to those quiet moments of restoration. It's a bit like pressing a reset button and rebooting the brain. And it makes a huge difference.

And how long did this take? Two minutes? Maybe three? And how do you feel now, with your mind that little bit clearer, calmer?

Taking control of your mind and body like this is an effective and easy way to let go of feeling overwhelmed, and overcome negative thoughts, fear, anxiety and stress.

This exercise is a great way to start controlling your mind and body; a great way to learn to program your mind to experience the world differently; to train your mind to do what *you want it to do*, so that you can feel calmer and cope better.

The beauty of this process is that you can do this for yourself.

I would recommend doing it at least four times a day:

- First thing in the morning when you wake

- Around lunchtime

- At sunset

- Just before you fall asleep

Of course, you can do it every hour or even every 20 minutes if you are having a particularly difficult day. This exercise will change your life… And your mind!

You will cope better, feel calmer, handle things more easily, get more done, and yet, have more energy left at the end of the day! The quality of your life will improve. Automatically you feel happier and more at peace. And when you feel happy and at peace, you will begin to manifest wonderful things, which brings more happiness and peace.

The bottom line is, that every time you do this, you are actively training your mind to do what you want it to do. An untrained mind is like a small child having a tantrum, you never know what's coming next! Taking control and training your mind is an important step in being able to manifest.

You see, when you have control of your mind, also you have control over what you manifest.

What else can you do to change your mindset for the better?

Become aware that everything you hear, every thought you have, is constantly changing your perceptions of yourself and your world. You are a work in progress. With every breath you take, every moment that passes, your mind is constantly assessing what you hear, see and experience. And as your mind processes new information, it is constantly updating the way you think, the way you feel, and the way you handle life. We are constantly changing and adapting, constantly making progress in one way or another. And progress is a powerful thing when it is headed in the right direction.

So, what else can you do, to take control of that direction?

The first step is to notice where your focus is.

What seeds are you planting into your mind today?

Your mind is a massive database of collected experiences and information about life. And this database is always looking for more information to update the *'library'* of the mind, to understand life better. The mind needs to understand life so that it can alert you to danger and suggest things to make you feel happy, safe and secure.

But the fact that your mind is constantly in *Live Record Mode* means that it records everything it hears indiscriminately. And an even bigger BUT is that your subconscious not only records life, but it also, as I mentioned in Chapter Two, cannot tell the difference between what is real and what is imagined. (Remember how when you imagined biting into a big juicy lemon, your mouth started to salivate?)

And what that means is that you need to take care of what you expose your mind to.

Imagined danger and the link to adrenaline

So, imagine now that you are watching a scary movie. Suddenly you find yourself holding your breath, and feeling anxious... Your heart starts pounding, and you might even start sweating and shaking. This is an indicator that your body is reacting to the scene in the movie by releasing adrenaline into your bloodstream.

The truth is, that when we are in danger, **real or perceived**, the body automatically pumps large doses of adrenaline into our bloodstream to help us '*defend*' ourselves. Adrenaline is also known as the '*fight or flight*' hormone.

Centuries ago, when we lived off the land and needed to defend ourselves against wild animals and invading tribes, we needed large doses of adrenaline to give us the strength to fight off the danger. Interestingly, physical activity, such as running, or fighting, burns up the huge amounts of adrenaline flooding our body during a time of danger.

But here's the problem: in our modern society, there are no wild animals and there are no invading tribes. We don't need those excessive amounts of adrenaline, because we are at home, perfectly safe, just watching a movie. And because you are not physically engaged in fighting off the danger, there is no way to release the trapped adrenaline.

This is a problem, and people react differently to this excess of unused adrenaline. Some people love the *adrenaline rush*... It can make you feel fearless, and bold, a powerful feeling which can be very addictive. This is why some people get hooked on extreme sports. And there's nothing wrong with that because the exercise from the sport naturally releases the adrenaline. It gets used up.

But when you are watching a scary movie in your home, the trapped adrenaline can easily transform into anxiety and fear. Anxiety is the brain's way of alerting you to a dangerous situation. And because the disaster on the screen is perceived as real, the anxiety and fear you feel are also very real.

To make matters worse, most of us, when experiencing anxiety, try our very best to ignore it. We've been trained, by our parents, peers and society, to suppress negative feelings. So, when we experience negative emotions, such as fear or anxiety, we feel embarrassed, cover it up and pretend that nothing is wrong.

But here's the thing... When you ignore the danger signals being transmitted through your body, your brain notices that you are not taking action. In response, it naturally triggers an even bigger release of adrenaline to get your attention. It wants to '*alert*' you to the '*danger*'. And the more unused adrenaline there is locked in your body, the more anxious you become. This can easily spiral out of control into a full-blown panic attack. And anyone who has ever had a panic attack or seen someone have one can confirm that the feeling of imminent doom feels very real too.

But not all adrenaline is bad for you. Adrenaline keeps you alert and gives you a burst of energy when you need it. But when your mind and body are constantly exposed to external factors that trigger huge bursts of adrenaline on an ongoing basis, this can become a problem, because the adrenal glands cannot keep up with the constant demand for adrenaline. This can lead easily to adrenal burnout.

I remember a client who came to see me with adrenal burnout. She was utterly exhausted and suffering from debilitating panic attacks, which struck randomly. She explained that she had a high-pressure job with long hours, was also a mother and wife and that she excelled at everything she did. She prided herself on being a superwoman.

'*I love it,*' she told me. '*I love the feeling of power I get from all the pressure! It makes me feel alive! I thrive on it!*'

But she wasn't thriving on it at all. The constant demand for more and more adrenaline from her body had completely depleted her adrenal glands. And her body was starting to say no. You see, when you have adrenal burnout, it starts to affect both your mental and physical health.

Adrenal fatigue is characterised by:

- Constant fatigue

- Brain fog

- Being unable to think clearly

- Depression

- Feeling overly sensitive, tearful and emotional

- Feeling overwhelmed

- Dizziness

- Panic attacks

In addition, when the adrenal glands are not producing enough adrenaline, there can be further health problems such as weight gain, high blood pressure, insomnia, and headaches. If the issue is not addressed and corrected, there can be long-term damage leading to more serious illness. For example, there is a very definite link between stress and cancer.

But the damage is not only physiological. It can also severely impact your state of mind, causing mental fatigue, anxiety, panic and fear, as the mind sends a signal through the body that *'Something is wrong...'*

Living in fear-state causes further problems as these emotions are highly charged with negativity, which is then transmitted outwards. So, The Law of Negative Attraction kicks in, as you start attracting fearful situations into your life.

So now you can begin perhaps to understand some of the reasons you are not able to get manifest good things, to work for you.

So, my advice is, don't binge on movies with violence, horror and crime. Yes, we are very resilient and not every single little thing we watch is going to cause a problem, but there needs to be a sense of balance. Make sure you set aside time to reset your mind, to slow everything down, to take time out to reset your brain.

And when you start to notice yourself going into anxiety or fearful states, or start worrying excessively, or notice yourself feeling unusually negative, that's the time to cut back.

One of the things I do, when I occasionally watch a movie or series with violence, is to mentally *'tune out'* while the violent scene is being enacted. I distract myself. I might play a game, or play with my pet, or message a loved one... And I make sure that I am 100% focussed on my *'distraction.'*

Choose what to expose your mind to. This is important.

Similarly, if you have unresolved trauma, are overwhelmed right now, or have a lot on your plate, or are an empath or sensitive to energy, I would advise avoiding these triggers altogether, at least until you feel more stable, and have a sense of control over your state of mind.

Treat your mind the way you would treat your very own child. Be gentle and caring. Love and nurture it. When you do this, the rewards are huge!

But movies are not the only negative influences on our mind...

Can singing a song with sad lyrics really affect my mind?

Oh yes... Very definitely. This might sound crazy but think for a moment about how you feel when you sing a sad song. Your emotions start to line up with the words in the song. Singing creates pictures, feelings and stories in our minds. And these stories are graphic descriptors that can impact the way our mind sees and experiences life.

When you sing, you are communicating directly with your subconscious. So, if you find yourself bellowing out the lyrics to heart-breaking sad songs, guess what? You're telling your subconscious that the world is a sad and heart-breaking place. And if your mind believes that the world is a sad and heart-breaking place, where partners cheat on each other, and relationships are full of pain, this will naturally reinforce this belief in your mind...

Do you really want to reinforce such a painful belief?

You do know that you are placing a direct order to The Universe: *'Send me more of this heart-breaking sadness that I am singing about...'*

It's not that your mind is sending out negative vibrations because it hates you. It's sending out negative vibrations because it doesn't understand that there's a choice of a different reality.

And I can tell you from experience, that it doesn't matter what you order! Whatever you order is exactly what you will attract. This is an unassailable fact, which I have discovered over many, many years of observation.

For example, if you are belting out the lyrics of an angry protest song... How do you feel? Angry. And when you feel angry, you are transmitting anger, which will naturally attract more things to make you angry. It's almost as if The Universe says: *'Ohh... I understand. You want to study the emotion of anger? Okay, I will send you more things to feel angry about.'*

Have you ever noticed that when you are frustrated and irritable, everything goes wrong? That's The Universe responding to your request to study the emotion of frustration and irritation. It's really simple, once you understand the principle.

So, take care of the words you sing with such passion. Even more so, if you are going through something tough, or are feeling emotionally fragile.

Rather compile a playlist of uplifting songs with powerful and beautiful lyrics. Sing at the top of your voice. Feel that power and joy filling you and bursting from you. Then you can be assured that you are on track and are attracting powerful and beautiful things into your life.

And what a beautiful and simple way to program your mind for a wonderful and joyful life!

What else can you watch out for? Bad news!

It's easy to get swept into *'wanting to know the truth'*. Of course, it's okay to check in on the news, but make sure you are being level-headed and objective. There is a difference between checking the news, and endlessly scrolling for bad news and horror stories. There is a word for this – It's called *'doom scrolling'*. And doom scrolling can easily lead to endlessly seeking out conspiracy theories, and you really don't want to go down that rabbit hole!

Be very aware of *'click-baiting'*. Don't allow these people to take away your power by frightening you so they can get more clicks. Don't go there. It leads to despair and fear, and that is the last thing you want to feel if you are setting out to manifest good things for yourself.

Negative people

As much as possible, avoid negative people and negative situations. If you do come across drama, anger, and trouble, as we all do, from time to time, resist the temptation to get involved! Negative people who create drama are looking to draw you in. They want you to react because once you react, they have an excuse to escalate the drama. And once the drama escalates, no one wins, least of all you. Rather be completely impassive.

My motto is, *'No reaction is the best reaction'*.

So if you are living or working in a bad situation, all the more reason to practice mindfulness; to bring yourself to that quiet place in your mind. Focus on creating that beautiful inner silence. The more you do this, the quieter your mind becomes, and the calmer the signals you are transmitting. You will be amazed at how quickly the drama will quite naturally disappear from your life. I've seen this happen in my own life.

There is another positive spin-off too. When you are in control of your mind and refuse to react or participate in negativity, the troublemakers become bored with baiting you, so they will move on, and look for their drama elsewhere.

Dwelling on negative situations

Try not to dwell too much on troubling situations. Negative focus is a mental *'hook'* that keeps you bound and connected to negativity. The more you react to a problem, the deeper the hook digs in. And the deeper the hook digs in, the more you will manifest more of the same.

One of the most powerful ways of effectively dealing with a negative situation is to imagine viewing it from above... To distance yourself from it. Become the observer. Quieten your mind. Be impartial and perhaps even mildly curious about the lesson you are learning from this experience.

And there are many lessons to be learned. Always remember that you created this situation to learn something.

So, here are the steps:

- Take responsibility

- Understand the lesson

- Let go and move on to better things

Does your mind loop endlessly in negativity?

- What thoughts do you think when you wake up in the morning?

- Do you find your mind focussing on trauma and heartache?

- Do you find your mind rehashing your problems endlessly?

Remember, the mind is a computer which loves solving problems. It wants to focus on problems. Train your mind instead, to focus on positivity.

The mind is exactly like a child. It doesn't *like* discipline and control, but it loves it!

When the mind is disciplined, controlled and given direction, it begins to understand what is required of it. And when it understands what is required of it, this gives it a sense of security. And a secure mind is a happy mind.

One last note about comparing the mind to a child, and it's one I find very amusing. The mind is exactly like a child in that it too, is very easily distracted. It is really easy to distract your mind from negativity.

'Look at the beautiful flower; isn't it a lovely day; the sun feels so warm on my skin; I love that girl's outfit... I wonder where she got it; what should I have for dinner this evening...' etc.

So, so easily distracted! And you can use this to your benefit! Distract your mind from negativity and fear. Chose to redirect and distract your thoughts. It's really easy!

The truth is, the more direction you give your mind, the happier it is. The result is that it starts to respond the way you want it to.

Isn't that beautiful and profound and ever so simple? Programming your own mind is really not that difficult, once you understand the principles.

The mind is exactly like a child, learning and experiencing and having fears. And you can help it and soothe it with a gentle heart, some discipline and control, and a little healthy distraction.

Distracting or redirecting the mind to create serenity, peace and joy
Beautiful exercises to activate positive emotions and happiness:

1. Activate a positive emotion: Go back in time and remember one of the happiest moments in your life. Imagine yourself there now and make it a rich, focused image. Enrich your senses: activate smell and taste... Feel the sunshine, smell the blossoms/sea salt... notice the weather... The temperature... Hear the sounds... Be there now.

   Feel those powerful emotions vibrating in your body... Joy, happiness, inner peace, a sense of safety and security, good times!

   Absorb the experience. Feel the sun on your body, the water on your skin... The joy... Feel it right down into your cells. Flood your mind with these positive strong sensations... Feel them becoming part of your brain and part of your being... Smile... Laugh...

2. Sing a beautiful song at the top of your voice, even if you can't hold a tune!

3. Did you know that you can program your emotions with your body posture? There is a powerful technique that many public speakers use to fill themselves with confidence before going onstage. It's called the 'Superwoman/Superman Pose'.

   And it goes like this: feet firmly on the ground slightly apart, your hands on your hips, shoulders back, chest out, head high... And I encourage you to do this now. See if you can hold this pose for 10 minutes... How do you feel now? As though you could conquer t

4. Smile... Just smile. This is a simpler version of the exercise above. Smiling releases feel-good hormones, and it's a very easy way to program your mind right now at this moment.

5. Remember, your mind cannot tell the difference between what is real and what is imagined. So, try imagining the most wonderful things coming your way, right here, right now.

   Just for fun!

PART THREE

LEARN TO MANIFEST

CHAPTER ELEVEN

Change Your Mind And You Change Your World

The Beginning: Getting It Right

Manifesting comes from the inside

Here I share the real magic which makes it easy to manifest your perfect life – even if you don't know what your perfect life looks like! Many manifesting books and courses advocate that you need to know what you want to manifest it. But, much like the endless affirmations, I found this to be completely untrue!

Isn't it awesome that you don't have to know exactly what you want in order to manifest great things for yourself? You see, the methods I teach in this book overcome the block of not knowing what you want. And my methods are easy, fun and they work!

But don't worry, if you do know what you want to manifest, my methods work just as well!

Learning to manifest amazing things in your life starts with manifesting happiness inside yourself. Creating a powerful, joyful state of happiness inside yourself is key to creating the life of your dreams. Your outer world reflects your inner world, not the other way round.

You can think of it this way – when you throw a pebble into a pond, the ripples start from the inside, not the outside. It's the same with manifesting. Change who you are inside... The good stuff then comes effortlessly.

One of the biggest misconceptions about life is that we can 'buy' happiness, or that we can only be happy if we have the perfect partner who can 'make' us happy, or get the perfect job, or have a successful business, or own the latest car. And while all these things are very desirable, and manifesting them is immense fun, they can't *make* you happy if you are miserable inside.

First, you need to create happiness inside you. Then you will be able to easily attract all the beautiful things you desire, and then they will add to joy and happiness, not be the cause of it. Do you see the difference? It starts with creating joy and happiness inside yourself.

The First Secret: Happiness Comes First

Something interesting happens when you create happiness inside yourself because when you are happy, you automatically also create a strong sense of self-worth. And when you have that strong sense of self-worth, you automatically manifest things which are in line with how much you value yourself.

It comes right back to what I was talking about in Chapter Four. Look around you now, and notice what you have created. Then start actively working on building yourself up, believing in yourself, being your own best friend, and elevating how much you value and care about yourself. Create inner peace, joy and a strong sense of self-worth. And watch how your life transforms in front of your eyes in a very short time.

This was the first secret I stumbled on, so many years ago. If you change your inner reality, your outer reality will change too.

Really it comes down to one thing. You want to be happy, right? Right. So I'm going to teach you to be happy. And when you are happy, guess what? The Universe will bring you things to make you even happier.

Now I am sure that many of you will groan at hearing this, saying perhaps, *'But how can I be happy in my present circumstances?'*

Well, I am here to tell you that things don't have to be perfect for you to be happy. No matter how tough things are, there are ways to supersede the toughest circumstances. I know, because I did it. When I first started to have such huge success with manifesting, my life was, quite literally, a nightmare.

But I am getting ahead of myself here. Let's turn back the clock to that one day – no actually, to that one moment – that changed my life forever.

How did I change my mind and my world?

Here is a step-by-step account of exactly what happened, and how I changed my mind – and my world.

If I look back, I can see that my life at that time consisted of waking in the morning under a black cloud of depression, going to a job I hated, putting up with endless drama at work, and coming home to an empty home at night (at the time I had resolved to spend two years being single).

To top all of that, six months earlier, I had lost my sister to cancer. She had spent five long painful years fighting the disease with endless chemo treatments, determined to beat it. But when she was diagnosed with an inoperable brain tumour, it was a matter of months before it was over. She was my best friend, the one person who had always been there for me, and she was gone.

So there I was, alone, very alone. I was also still in the grip of intense blaming and anger about my childhood. Life was miserable, and I was deeply angry and unhappy about the injustice of it all. It just wasn't fair!

'Why me?' I lamented over and over. I felt so sorry for myself! I was miserable and bored with it all. Miserable and bored, and bored and miserable. I was so over it! There had to be a way to make life better.

So once again I turned my attention to manifesting. But all the manifesting techniques I'd been studying for so many years, still didn't work for me. Affirmations bored me to tears and left me feeling frustrated, unfulfilled and mentally and physically exhausted. So much hard work with zero results, and oh so boring! I just couldn't do it! And it didn't work for me anyway!

Next, I tried visualisation.

'Wouldn't it be wonderful,' I thought, *'To own a red sports car... Like a Ferrari or a Porsche.'*

I could almost see my conscious mind rolling on the floor in laughter at this crazy suggestion.

'That's ridiculous and far-fetched,' it was quick to tell me. *'How do you think you're ever going to have a red sports car? Let's do the math: you earn X and a red sports car costs Z! Even if you saved every penny you earned, you would still never have enough to buy that red sports car!'*

I tried the imagination technique: *'Feel it as if you already have it! Imagine how it feels to drive that red sports car... Feel the wind blowing through your hair... Smell that new car smell...'*

My conscious mind's answer to all this imagining stuff was swift and to the point. *'You're a dreamer. Always have been, always will be... Dream on, because that's all that red sports car will ever be... A dream.'*

Next, I tried the gratitude technique: naming the good things in my life. But it's difficult to be grateful when you are miserable.

Then I tried to name it: imagining the things that would make me happy. But that was a tall order too. I was not happy. End of story.

I tried to visualise how it would feel to be happy; to have my perfect life. But trying to decide exactly what my perfect life would look like was impossible. I didn't have a clue what would make me happy. I was far too deeply entrenched in my misery to even imagine what such a life what it might look like.

I quite literally couldn't see the wood for the trees. I was overwhelmed, grief-stricken, unhappy, frustrated and angry. And I didn't have the faintest idea of what I wanted. If someone had asked me, what would your perfect life look like, I could not have answered. I didn't know.

'What do I want?' I asked myself in desperation, over and over again. I drew a complete blank. I didn't know.

There were only two things I was clear about:

1. I knew I wanted to start a hypnotherapy practice, but it seemed as far-fetched as the red sports car!

2. I wanted to be happy but had no idea what would make me happy.

I had to face facts. My life was an endless misery and I had no idea what to do from here. I felt as if I'd been painted into a corner, with no way out. Trapped.

But feeling trapped forced me to dig deeper, and that was when I realised that I had quite literally created everything in my life... The drama, the misery, the bad luck... I was the ***one common denominator.***

I was struck by the irony of it all, that I had been battling for years to understand manifesting, and all along I had been manifesting! The only thing was, I had manifested misery by being miserable!

I remember the day very clearly. It was early autumn. The weather was just the way I liked it... Not too hot and not too cold. I was lucky because I had a lovely sunny office, and sometimes I'd stand in the sun to warm up.

And on that day, at that moment, I stood up and walked over to the patch of sun in my office, my mind mulling over the possibilities of this new information being true.

'If I created this mess with my misery,' I pondered, *'I wonder what would happen if I change the way I think and the way I feel?'*

But how? I had to face facts… I was anything but happy! How could I be happy, if I wasn't?

I could see no simple solution, so I allowed myself to just enjoy that spot of sunshine in my office for a few moments… As I connected with the warmth of the sun on my skin, I felt my mind go calm and still. And just for a moment, a tiny split second, I was happy.

'Wouldn't it be wonderful to feel this happy all the time?' I pondered.

And that's when it occurred to me. *'I wonder what would happen if I pretended to be happy all the time?'*

Studying hypnosis had taught me a lot about the human mind and how it worked, and it had quickly become my new favourite topic. One of the things that fascinated me is that the subconscious mind cannot tell the difference between what is real and what is imagined. So, I reasoned, if I could not actually **be happy**, because of the misery in my life, maybe, just maybe, I could **pretend to be happy**?

What if I could fool my own mind into believing that I was happy? I knew it was not going to be easy. But if it worked, it would be amazing!

I was blown away by the concept, and curious to see the results. So I started my experiment. I started to *pretend* to be happy.

The first three days were intense and extremely difficult. The negative thought patterns which were entrenched in my brain were a huge part of my life. But I was determined to give this experiment my all, and I persisted in eradicating negativity from my mind. I made a pact to stop criticising and judging everything and everyone; to stop finding fault everywhere. I started to realise how nothing had satisfied me; nothing had been good enough and nothing made me happy... which explained why I didn't know what would make me happy!

I started observing my own mind, determined to break the negative patterns of anger, blame and self-pity. I watched my thoughts like a sentinel guarding a castle. The moment a negative thought popped into my mind, I imagined myself pulling it out like a weed, and throwing it away.

As I observed my patterns, I began to learn and understand more about myself. When I felt myself getting upset, or reacting to something negative that happened, I focused on my breathing... Nothing but my breath... Intentionally quieting my mind... Stilling my thoughts... Deliberately distracting myself from negative and painful thoughts.

I started to slow down my racing thoughts, and consciously slow down time, so I felt more in control.

I stopped judging others. And myself. I began to be gentle and kind to myself, and think supportive and loving thoughts.

I focused on the beauty of this world; the scent of blossoms in the air; the feel of a breeze against my cheek; the joy of stroking the silky fur of my cat and listening to her rumbling purr; the colours in the sky at dawn and sunset; a scented candle; rose petals in my bath…

I learned that the mind is easily distracted, and therefore easily managed.

When I woke in the morning, I would instantly redirect my mind from the misery of my life to focus on the birds singing outside my window and how beautifully they sang.

'What a beautiful day!' I would tell myself.

On heavy days when I woke under a black cloud of depression, I would sing to myself a tune I was taught as a child.

'If you're happy and you know it, clap your hands…' And yes, I would clap my hands! *'If you're happy and you know it and you really want to show it, if you're happy and you know it, clap your hands!'* Clap clap…

I was quite literally rewiring my own brain.

The results were mind-blowing and exceeded my wildest expectations. Within three days of *'pretending'* to be happy, my world started to change in every way imaginable. It was that fast!

The first thing I noticed was that on the third day, I woke up feeling happy. I no longer had to pretend to be happy, because I was happy. This was a new feeling and it surprised me. It would appear that by pretending to be happy, my brain had started producing its own endorphins! I was amazed and thrilled.

'This is crazy!' I thought. *'How can it be true?'* But it was, and I was loving it!

But waking up happy wasn't the only thing that was crazy, because everything around me started to change too. My depression lifted and I felt more at peace with life. Circumstances at work eased up. The drama which had dogged me for so long simply faded away. I couldn't believe it!

Inspired by these wonderful results, I began to imagine what else might change in my life. I imagined a huge set of cogwheels, like wooden gears, interlocked and linked to each other, turning. And as the wheels turned, they were bringing more good things into my life.

I was filled with anticipation, wondering what these wonderful things might be, that were coming my way. I imagined circumstances shifting, changing and the wooden gears locking into place to make great things come my way... I couldn't wait to see what would happen next!

One night I went outside to admire the night sky. It was a beautiful evening with a clear star-studded sky. Some instinct, or maybe it was the playfulness that I had begun to manifest in my life, inspired me. I threw my head back, and opened my arms to the night sky. *'I don't know what I want,'* I said out loud playfully. *'But I know you know. I know that you know what will make me happy. Bring that. Bring that...'*

It felt wonderful to surrender, to trust, to hand over control. I realised that I had been trying to control everything my entire life! And it felt amazing to just let go.

I can remember going to sleep that night feeling really calm. I knew that I had opened myself up and let go of controlling... I had taken my will out of the equation. I had surrendered.

And I waited with a sense of curiosity and a slight amusement... Wondering what would come of it... What would happen...

Somehow, instinctively, I knew I'd been heard. I could literally feel the response. And I knew that whatever was coming, was going to be amazing! It gave me goosebumps thinking about it!

And something did happen. A lot of things happened! So many things happened that it blew my mind!

Within a couple of weeks, I met a fellow hypnotist at a meeting. This young man knew a lot about building websites, and also a lot about online advertising. And he just happened to be running a weekend course the following weekend. The synchronicity was astounding, and I knew instinctively that our meeting was no accident.

I took his course, went home and put together my website. I did online research and learned more ways to market my website. I worked hard, determined to make the most of the gifts I had been given. And it started to pay dividends. Clients started booking.

I was thrilled and started playing even more with techniques. I started to pretend I already had a full-time practice...

I would walk into my *'consulting room'*, which at the time was nothing more than a spare room in my house I had converted. I would joyfully throw open the curtains, open my arms wide, and say out loud, 'I am fully booked for the whole month... I have six clients booked every day.' And I would send that beautiful message out with the full expectation of it becoming my new reality.

In December when I went on leave from my day job, I found myself fully booked for the entire two weeks! By the time I went back to work, I was working two jobs. And my hypnosis practice kept growing and growing...

By the end of January, I was exhausted and knew I couldn't keep up the double jobs... So I took a leap of faith and resigned from my corporate day job. I was thrilled and not the least bit nervous. The end of February couldn't come soon enough!

Finally, the day came to say goodbye to regular employment and start my real life. I opened my full-time practice on the 1st of March 2013. And I've never looked back!

The Universe lined up perfectly with my expectations. I rented a stunning office in a great location (another gift from The Universe). The bookings continued to pour in. It wasn't long before my words came true... I was seeing six clients a day, six days a week, just as I had imagined when I was on leave in December, seeing clients in my spare room.

I was living my dream, and it felt amazing!

After all the years and years of studying the Law Of Attraction, I had finally stumbled onto something that worked! And still, my business continued to grow and grow.

In March, my first month of full-time practice, *I matched my corporate salary*. I actually earned slightly more than my corporate salary, in that first month. I was astounded!

Encouraged by my success, I started playing with a new technique. I started to imagine a huge Christmas tree, its massive boughs almost bending under the weight of beautifully wrapped gifts. *'I don't know what's in those gifts, but I know it's going to be amazing!'* I told myself.

The sense of anticipation was so intense it gave me goosebumps! By now, I knew that this would bring even more beautiful things into my life, and I couldn't wait to see what was coming next.

And it did come.

Within a couple of months of opening my business, I was approached by a well-known magazine. They wanted to feature my hypnosis weight-loss program.

The weird thing was, that a few months earlier when I was still in my corporate job and was seeing clients after hours, I had one day thought to myself, *'Wouldn't it be fun to be featured in a magazine...'*

And here I was... Being featured in a magazine.

The article brought me even more clients. Life kept getting better and better!

Soon after that, I was approached to appear on radio, and then on TV. I was thrilled! It was all such fun!

Surprisingly, I had no fear whatsoever of appearing on TV as I had, by then, developed a childlike joy of exploration and trust, which made the whole process an immense amount of fun.

I discovered something new about myself… I loved being interviewed on TV! I was passionate about hypnosis and I knew my subject, and I felt completely at ease in front of the cameras. This was such a surprise to me, because as a child I had an intense fear of public speaking, and I did not enjoy being in the spotlight at all!

As one TV presenter put it, *'You're a natural.'* I could hardly believe that the lost girl from a few months ago, the girl who had manifested so much continuing trauma, had now manifested this!

But the weird thing was, that it felt right! It was strangely calming and reassuring. It felt as if this was meant to be… As if it had always been meant to be. I was meant to study The Law Of Attraction… I had been pushed into that corner until I felt trapped and couldn't bear it anymore, and was forced to find a way out.

Suddenly I understood that everything bad that had ever happened to me, had led me to this moment, this magnificent discovery. It all made sense. And it was awesome!

Each day became an adventure of expectation of good things coming my way. I became optimistic and filled with a deep sense of trust… Trust in myself, trust in life and absolute unshakable trust in the future.

It was like a fairy godmother took her magic wand and touched every part of my life. Except I was my own fairy godmother.

The really interesting thing is, that not once did I go looking for these amazing media opportunities... They came to me, as if by magic.

And life is magic if you can allow yourself to believe in magic. And even if you don't believe in magic, you can always pretend to believe in magic!

So here is what I learned from *'pretending'*:

- You don't have to be happy to become happy

- You can fool your brain into believing anything with your imagination

- The mind is easily distracted, and therefore easily managed

- When your brain believes you are happy, your body responds by creating more endorphins naturally

- After a while, it will no longer be necessary to pretend to be happy, because once your brain is creating endorphins, it will automatically continue to produce more and more endorphins... On its own

- You don't have to know what your perfect life looks like to start manifesting

- When you are living your life with a sense of adventure and an expectation of *amazing things coming your way*, life becomes an abundant adventure filled with **amazing things that keep coming your way!**

And one last note:

To add the cherry on the top of that first year of opening my brand new practice, going from a corporate job into my own business... As I mentioned earlier, in the first month I equalled my corporate salary, which was amazing. But there was more to come...

Within five months, I tripled my corporate salary!

So much for the so-called *'real world'* out there.

So much for everyone telling me, *'Don't give up your day job.'*

So much for the naysayers who told me, *'Stop dreaming...You cannot make a living from being a hypnotist...'*

My take on that would be to encourage you to dream your dreams. Make them happen. Watch them come true Because reality does not work the way we think it does! You create your reality with your mind, with your emotions, and with your thoughts!

I wonder how your life would change if you allowed yourself to start dreaming and actually believe your dreams, instead of the stuff we call 'real' in this world.

If my world could change so much in such a short time, I wonder how quickly your world could change too?

Maybe, you might think to yourself, *'It can't be as easy as this… my life is different… I am different.'*

But don't worry, I have your back because, in the next chapter, I'm going to give you some powerful ways to shift your mind too. If there's one thing I've learned from 10 years of working with clients, it's that everyone can change if they want to!

There is a beautiful quote, and it goes like this: *If nothing ever changed, there would be no butterflies.*

I love that!

Change is possible, and yes, you can change.

It's really simple: Change Your Mind, and You Change Your Life!

CHAPTER TWELVE

Let's Make It Happen

Fall In Love With Life And Life Will Fall In Love With You

Since that beautiful autumn day 10 years ago, I have played with and mastered many techniques of manifesting. And I continue to develop new processes daily, keen to learn even more. It is a fascinating subject, and I never get bored exploring new processes.

So read through the methods, and then play with them... Have fun. See what works for you. One thing is certain: there are an infinite number of ways to attract what you desire.

Playfulness and pretend happiness

Of course, this was the first manifesting success technique I stumbled onto, and I've often wondered what it is about this technique that works so well...

And I don't know if it is the state of happiness, pretend or real, that attracts things to make you even happier, or if it's that happiness is a vibration which, when transmitted outwards, magnetically attracts wonderful things naturally. Either way, it works!

So let's talk about some of the methods I use to make me feel so ecstatically joyfully alive and happy.

Start the day with an expectation of wonderful things coming your way

So, first thing in the morning, go to your window, throw open the curtains, blinds or windows... Then open your arms to welcome the day, and say out loud, *'What a beautiful day! I can't wait to see what this day brings... There's something amazing coming... I just know it!'*

Feeling the anticipation of something amazing on its way to you magnetises your mind to automatically attract the most magical things. The higher the vibration, the better it works!

One of my clients told me an amusing story. He was doing this routine one morning when his six-year-old son walked into the room.

'What are you doing, Daddy?' the little boy asked curiously.

His dad laughed and said, *'I'm imagining a wonderful day because when I do that it makes me happy, and when I'm happy, great things happen in my day!'*

'Ohhh...' His son responded with wide eyes. *'So if I do that, will I also have a good day?'*

'Of course!' his dad responded. *'Let's do it together.'*

When he told me this story, it made my day! Imagine if we trained our children to expect miracles instead of disasters! It would change the world! So why not encourage your children to expect the best out of life? For centuries we have been taught to fear life! That's crazy, and it needs to change!

So, why not teach your children to start attracting a wonderful life for themselves? It definitely can't do any harm, and if a problem does come up in their day, their powerful positive state of mind will help them to handle it so much better.

But I digress, so let's get back to you, because this is important, and you are important!

Mantras or Affirmations

When I first started my business, my morning mantra was: 'I have six clients a day six days a week! I'm really successful, and it's awesome! I'm loving it!'

This technique was incredibly powerful. At the time, I was only seeing one to two clients a day! So I started this mantra as a game, an experiment, but it wasn't long before more and more people started booking. Imagine my joy and surprise when I successfully manifested six clients a day six days a week! And it happened incredibly quickly.

So start creating your mantra for your needs and desires today. Play and have fun. Tap into the anticipation, expectation and excitement...

There are two things to be aware of when creating mantras:

Create your mantra in the present tense... As if it is already here!

- Wrong: 'I'm going to be so happy when my business has grown and I have lots of new clients.'

- Right: 'My client base is growing really fast, and I'm loving being so busy! I even have a waiting list!'

- Wrong: 'I'll be happy when I have met the perfect person.'

- Right: 'I'm in a beautiful relationship with the perfect partner, and I'm loving it!'

Avoid negativity in your mantras.

- Wrong: 'This job sucks. I hate it. I want a new job.'

- Right: 'I've just been offered the job of my dreams! I'm so excited! I can't wait to start!'

- Wrong: 'I'm never going to meet the right person. All the good ones are taken.'

- Right: 'I have attracted the most amazing partner and they are perfect for me!'

- Wrong: 'It's difficult to start your own business. The odds are against you.'

- Right: 'I have my own business and I'm thriving!'

You see, it doesn't matter if it is not true. It only matters that you imagine how it feels when it is true!

One word of caution: you need to be a little bit practical. Don't be expecting a million dollars to magically appear in your bank overnight, or to find a bag of money on your doorstep.

If you desire financial freedom, put yourself into a state of expectation of creating wealth for yourself, and you will manifest ways and ideas to create that wealth. And if you allow The Universe to guide you, it will show you the way, and the rewards will be phenomenal.

Imagine the surprise and joy you feel when the most astonishing events, synchronicities, and coincidences start appearing in your life like magic; where destiny seems to deliver magical gifts, surprises, circumstances, opportunities and people directly into your sphere of existence; when the most unbelievable crazy things start happening. Where you can start to connect to your path… Find direction… As if someone were leading you by the hand…

So open yourself up to possibilities and change. Notice the signs and signals which will help you to connect to a wonderful and deeply fulfilling life, where financial rewards are automatically part of the deal!

Don't know what you want to manifest? No problem!

Even if you don't have a clear vision of what you want to manifest, say out loud (even if it sounds and feels crazy):

*'I don't know what is coming, but I know it's amazing... I can **feel** it coming... I can't wait to see what it is...'*

And feel the anticipation of something amazing coming your way... Even if you don't have a clue what it is!

I like to go outside and open my arms to The Universe / God / Energy / Life / Your Higher Self and say these magical words: *'I don't know what I want, but I know that you know what will make me happy... Bring that... Bring that...'*

I love this technique because you are taking your will out of the equation. You are trusting that the best life will be given to you. And that trust opens doors you could not have imagined!

So let go of trying to control everything... Allow yourself to surrender and trust and receive the exact right things for you... Just for you!

Not naming it is all about surrender and trust

I think that one of our biggest problems in life is trying to control everything around us. And of course, when you have been through trauma, trying to control everything is a way to try and feel safe. It's a normal human response to having been hurt in any way.

But tuning in to abundance is all about learning to let go; to trust again. And here's the thing: it's not about trusting the world, or people, or anything else. It's about trusting yourself. All trust issues stem from being fearful and not trusting ourselves. It's that simple.

But if you think about it, the fact that you have been through so much, and have learned so much, means you are the best and most qualified person to look after you. So you can trust yourself because you know you can handle anything that comes your way.

You are not that little child anymore, who had no control over their life, you're not that vulnerable younger version of yourself anymore, who got taken for a fool, or made mistakes. And actually, I really dislike the word mistake... It's all wrong. If you think about it, how else do we learn, but by making 'so-called '*mistakes*'? They should actually be called '*learnings*'.

And when you made those so-called bad decisions, those '*mistakes*', you learned. And when you learn, you become strong, amazing, powerful and wise. And when you are wise, you learn that you can trust yourself.

Remember the wisdom that comes from your GIFT: *Great Insights From Trauma*. And you can rely on those GIFTs to keep you safe; to help you make good decisions; to draw the necessary boundaries.

When you trust yourself, you feel calm because you know you have all the resources you need to make good decisions. Trusting yourself is all about choosing to make good decisions. And when you make good decisions, you build trust in yourself, and you feel safe. And when you feel safe, you no longer need to control anything.

And then it becomes easy to go with the flow, to open yourself to abundance, to surrender to The Universe / God /Your Higher Self, and say, '*I know you know what will make me happy. Bring me that…*'

Also, similarly, '*All my needs are taken care of.*' is a beautiful mantra.

'*I am abundantly blessed…*' And feel it in your cells!

'*I am loved and protected and nurtured…*' And believe it! Feel safe; feel protected; feel loved.

And the beauty of it is, that if you believe you are protected and taken care of, you are! All you need to do is believe!

Magic doors

Play with your imagination: picture a set of double doors magically opening for you, perhaps you can see yourself stepping through, or maybe, when you open those doors, magical opportunities start flowing towards you. You don't even have to know what is behind those doors, just know that it's something so astoundingly amazing that it takes your breath away!

If you do know what you want, see yourself doing the things you want to do, and receiving the things you want in your life. Feel how it feels to have those things. The more you do this, the faster things will change. Staggering, jaw-dropping coincidences and opportunities will start to appear in your life, as if by magic!

Create your own images and ideas which give you those awesome goosebumps! Goosebumps are an amazing way to invoke that high vibration, that frequency of anticipation and excitement.

Happiness dairy

Many manifesting books advocate keeping a gratitude diary, but I prefer a happiness diary. A happiness diary is different in that it encourages you to focus on things that make you happy.

They don't even need to be actual events! You could even say something like, *'Today I woke with a powerful feeling of joy… I just know that everything is going to be okay, and that amazing things are coming my way.'*

Use your Happiness Diary to set intentions at the beginning of your day, such as: *'I choose to see the best in everyone and everything today.'*

This is a very effective way of transforming negative thinking into an expectation of attracting wonderful things. And even if your situation in your life is difficult and challenging, you're still programming your mind by setting the intention, by choosing to notice the good in the world. And the more good you notice, the more your mind accepts that the world is a joyful place, and so it will automatically attract powerfully positive things to confirm this new belief.

Another great thing to do is to reflect on good things that happened during your day. Consider, what was amazing about this day? Or what was the best thing about today? And write that down.

Or, *'I was walking in the mall and decided to smile, and people started smiling back. It felt like I had spread a little love in the world, and that felt great!'*

Or, *'I took a moment to just enjoy the feeling of the sun warming my skin, and it brought me a lot of inner peace.'*

It helps to shift the mind into that powerful happiness experience so that this becomes a permanent way of looking at life. It changes your perspective on life.

Be sure to write down your manifesting successes as well. This is empowering and encouraging. It boosts the belief that you can manifest great things for yourself, that you are a successful manifester, and that you can be confident of manifesting more amazing things for yourself!

What is the difference between a happiness diary and a gratitude diary?

A happiness diary is very different from a gratitude diary. A happiness diary lists the things that make you happy. A gratitude diary is where you list the things you are grateful for, such as:

'I'm grateful that I have a great job / partner / home / car / business…'

However, I have reservations about the gratitude diary:

1. It can become repetitive, and anything repetitive can become a burden, which can cause resentment and frustration.

2. Saying thank you for every single little thing can have the reverse effect, where you start to feel guilty for having these things, which can lead to a feeling you don't deserve them. And that is the opposite of what we are doing here.

But there is a place for gratitude, and when I manifest something truly awesome, I often say thank you, and the feeling here is pure joy, which is a beautiful vibration to be able to manifest more wonderful things.

Gratitude at the end of a beautiful day, where everything was just perfect, is also good. This is an ideal time to be grateful.

So, to sum it up, spontaneous gratitude works well, but repetitive gratitude can become a burden.

By the way, writing in the old-fashioned way, with a pen and paper works best. The movements of your hand on the paper mentally and physically connects the words on the page to your subconscious mind, and so this is a powerful way to program your mind directly.

Affirmations

If you want to use affirmations, there are a few ways to do this.

You can repeat them to yourself over and over. I'm not a fan of this method, as I find it boring and frustrating, and negative emotions such as boredom and frustration actually block manifesting! No wonder it wasn't working for me!

So I devised some other techniques.

Write down your affirmations

The most important factor here is that you need to write your affirmations by hand, with a pen and paper, as with the *happiness and gratitude diary*.

Write your affirmations on post-it notes, and stick them in unexpected places, such as, on the inside of your cupboard door, on the fridge door, on the bathroom mirror… The constant reminders will feed your mind and program your intentions.

If you have a single particular thing you want to manifest, you can write out that one sentence 20 times every day – just before bed is a good time as your mind will be processing the information while you sleep. Early morning is also good, as your mind is fresh and alert. You are quite literally programming your mind to transmit the signals which will attract these circumstances to manifest your desires.

Remember it has to be with pen and paper. Typing the words on a keypad just doesn't do it.

A powerful mantra - 'I am enough'

To give your self-esteem a powerful boost, write these three words: 'I am enough.'

It's a beautiful thing to write, to feel good about yourself, especially for those of you who doubt yourself or are low on confidence. Entire books have been written about the power of these three simple words.

It is not only empowering, but also enhances a feeling that you deserve good things.

I wrote it on my dressing table mirror, and every day when I woke up, those words were right there, in front of me, and I can attest to the power of these words. They shifted me in a beautiful way.

Walk the walk

Using physiology to manifest your dreams is a very cool technique. Did you know that the body produces specific chemicals in the body, in response to your posture, how you stand, how you walk, and how you talk...? This is called physiology, and it's a fascinating study.

There is a very well-known exercise that public speakers use before they go onstage. And it consists of the Superwoman Pose (or Superman Pose, for the guys). The pose consists of standing feet apart firmly on the ground in line with the hips, chest out, head high, and hands on hips.

And before they go on stage, the public speaker will hold this pose for a full 10 minutes. In response to this posture, the brain physically pumps feel-good hormones and chemicals through the body. These chemicals and hormones boost self-confidence, calmness and a feeling of being completely in control.

And you can use it too. It's a great way to pump up your confidence before going into an interview, an important meeting, or a sales pitch... It's truly amazing how awesome you feel afterwards. Why not try it now, just for fun?

So if you can boost confidence with the Superman/Superwoman pose, then it stands to reason that you can also use physiology to *connect to how it feels as if you had already manifested your dreams!*

So how would it *feel* to be a millionaire? How would it *feel* to have the perfect job, the perfect partner, a hugely successful business, and financial security?

When I was manifesting my business, I often used to *'practice'* walking as if I were a very successful businesswoman. I would often think to myself, *'My business is booming... I have so many clients... Money is pouring into my bank... I am so abundant... So happy... So joyful... It feels great to be successful!'*

So start playing with this technique today. Align yourself with how it would feel if you already had the thing you desire. Feel it in your body and mind, the excitement, the joy, that moment when you *already have it* in your life.

Walk the walk. Feel that abundance in your cells... In your veins... Remember, the subconscious mind cannot tell the difference between what is real and imagined, and by feeling abundant you are quite literally activating abundance!

If you want to attract the perfect partner, walk like you love you and care for you... As if you are special... because guess what? You are!

The more you feel it, walk it, talk it, live it, dream it, become it, the higher the vibration, the more powerfully you are attracting incredible and extraordinary things into your life.

Dream big! Dream wild!

Finding the balance

During this initial stage of adjusting to happiness, I found it important to balance these intense states of excitement and anticipation, with times of inner peace and tranquillity.

I was quite literally rewiring my brain and my brain sometimes rebelled against the changes. Sometimes the excitement spiralled into anxiety and the old fears would crowd my mind. How could this be real? Would it last? Was it safe to believe that life could change so much?

So, to quieten the insecurities of my mind, I used a lot of techniques to calm my mind... To retrain my brain to stop expecting disasters!

One of the most powerful of these is to practice the simple art of living in the moment. Slow time down... Take a moment to just breathe... Be in silence... Notice the blue of the sky... And when was the last time you looked at cloud shapes? Notice the feeling of the sun on your skin; the breeze on your cheek; the scent of flowers drifting in the air; a beautiful sunset...

I often set my alarm to wake extra early, before sunrise, to watch the sky turn from black to blue, pink and crimson, with a nice cup of hot coffee warming my hands…

Watching the sunrise gives a feeling of intense calmness but also the anticipation and joy of a new day dawning. I find sunrise a beautiful and balancing experience. There's something about that early morning air, the birds starting to welcome the day with their songs… I've noticed that birds sing the best and loudest first thing in the morning. There's something very uplifting hearing their joyful song welcoming the day.

But of course, nature is not everyone's thing, and that is also okay. Find your own ways to calm your mind. Have a candlelit bath, burn incense, set aside time for prayer, meditate, do yoga, go for a walk, book a massage, a manicure, a weekend away with your loved one, or a weekend away alone (I can highly recommend that! It's fun, balancing, beautiful and empowering!).

Make time to listen to inspiring speakers, read a good book, spend time with a loved one, spend time with you… We so often neglect spending time alone. Find the balance; set aside the time to nurture yourself, in whatever makes you feel good.

This is important. You are important! You wouldn't be here reading this book if it weren't important to you and if *You* weren't important to you.

Many things are deeply nourishing to the mind and soul, and bring about a sense of inner peace. And cultivating that inner peace is where you find the balance and a deep sense of connecting to how much you care about yourself.

And that is a beautiful thing.

CHAPTER THIRTEEN

Getting The Very Best Out Of Your Life

Transform Yourself - Transform Your World!

PART ONE: TRANSFORMING LIMITING BELIEFS

With every limiting belief we have, there is a corresponding *lesson to be learned*. And when you dig that little bit deeper to find the lesson and process the lesson, you redefine who you are. And when you have understood the lesson, you can move on to create the shift.

Common limiting beliefs:

- Nothing good lasts

- Money doesn't grow on trees

- The rich get richer and the poor get poorer

SO, LET'S START WITH NOTHING GOOD LASTS

There could be several lessons connected to this belief:

- I don't trust the world

- I don't trust people

- Bad things always happen to me

- I'm not good enough

- I'm much better at giving than receiving

Let's see what the lessons here could be:

I DON'T TRUST THE WORLD

- **Deeper understanding:** My trust was broken in the past.

- **Learning:** Things went wrong in the past, but I survived them and I am stronger and wiser and I learned that I can handle anything.

- **Lesson:** I let go of negativity, and choose to be playful with life.

- **New belief:** I love life and all the amazing things which keep coming my way!

I DON'T TRUST PEOPLE

- **Deeper understanding:** People have let me down in the past.

- **Learning:** Some people have problems, and act badly. That just means those people have problems.

- **Lesson:** I free myself from taking on other people's problems.

- **New belief:** Many people do good deeds, this shows that there are many good people in the world.

BAD THINGS ALWAYS HAPPEN TO ME

- **Deeper understanding:** Things that happened in the past were painful. Now I don't trust anything, and I feel fearful.

- **Learning:** The past has passed, it's time to let it go and move on.

- **Lesson:** Good things happen too, and the more I focus on the positive, the more positive things I attract into my life.

- **New belief:** This is where things get better... I can't wait to see what the future holds for me!

I'M NOT GOOD ENOUGH

- **Deeper understanding:** I haven't always believed in myself and put myself down a lot. I expect myself to be perfect and when I fail, I'm hard on myself.

- **Learning:** I choose to be gentle with myself and start supporting myself. I believe in myself.

- **Lesson:** I appreciate and love myself.

- **New belief:** I'm free to be myself and enjoy all aspects of who I am.

I AM MUCH BETTER AT GIVING THAN RECEIVING

- **Deeper understanding:** As a child, I was taught not to ask. Every time I asked I was made to feel guilty. Now I don't like asking or receiving because it makes me feel as if I owe a debt.

- **Learning:** I choose to let go of the guilt of asking for and receiving lovely things.

- **Lesson:** I give myself permission to receive.

- **New belief:** I care about myself and deserve beautiful things. It's fun to get stuff – I love it! I'm excited about the future!

MONEY DOESN'T GROW ON TREES

- **Deeper understanding:** When I was a child there was never enough money. My parents told me, 'Money doesn't grow on trees.' This made me feel guilty and formed a belief that there is not enough money.

- **Learning:** I experience fear and guilt when I think about having a lot of money.

- **Lesson:** The Universe is abundant… There is plenty for everyone.

- **New belief:** I love attracting abundance into my life. It's fun to see my bank balance growing. I love practising my manifesting skills in giving myself financial freedom.

THE RICH GET RICHER AND THE POOR GET POORER

- **Deeper understanding:** When I see someone driving a flashy car, it reminds me of how little I have, and it upsets me. Life doesn't feel fair. Why do other people have all the money? You need to have connections to make a lot of money.

- **Learning:** I'm becoming aware of how I jump to conclusions about other people's lives. I need to rethink this. I don't know how they made their money, or even how much money they have. Outward appearances can be deceiving.

- **Lesson 1:** I choose to focus on my own growth and my own beliefs about money. Money brings me security and financial freedom, which feels amazing!

- **Lesson 2:** Money is good. I can do a lot of wonderful things to make the world a better place when I have a lot of money. I can support charities, or perhaps create a trust fund to help educate someone deserving, and I can improve the lives of my family and my friends.

- **Lesson 3:** Money is fun. It brings great experiences, travel, shopping, my own home, a new car, and eating out!

- **Lesson 4:** I deserve wonderful things; I have a right to look after myself and to enjoy life. I love creating abundance and financial security for myself. Life gets better and better, and I'm loving it!

New belief: I am allowed to enjoy money! Life is meant to be fun, and it's fun creating money!

Here are two classic limiting beliefs:

- I'm unlucky in love

- I will never amount to anything

I want to talk about these fascinating aspects of life in more depth because they are important. Our relationships and our careers are two key factors in our overall happiness.

UNLUCKY IN LOVE

If you have had trouble attracting a good partner in the past, the chances are that you previously found yourself in the wrong types of relationships.

This can easily happen if:

You come from a background of childhood trauma, where your parents were poor role models

You have a lack of belief in yourself

You were not acknowledged as a child and feel that you don't deserve love

You were young and inexperienced and made poor partner choices

Maybe your thoughts went something like this: '*I'm so lucky to have someone interested in me, so I'd better jump at this opportunity. Why would anyone want me anyway? It's better to have someone rather than no one…*'

So you made a poor choice. But a poor choice can become a bad habit, and bad habits become limiting beliefs. And limiting beliefs, as we know by now, attract negative options. And when you have only negative options in front of you, you believe that you have no choice.

I'm here to tell you that you do have a choice. So start exercising that choice, and when those *bad apples* appear, just say no! Don't settle!

And yes, The Universe could test you by sending more bad apples until you have observed, learned and understood your patterns of the past.

It's almost as if The Universe is saying, '*Are you sure you don't want another bad apple?*'

So you need to have faith, stay strong and keep saying no. You need to stand your ground, and tell yourself, '*There is someone much better for me.*' And keep saying it until you believe it!

Saying no is all about learning to love yourself, honour yourself and support yourself.

So be sure to tell yourself: '*I deserve a wonderful partner, and the world is full of wonderful people looking to meet someone just like me.*'

It comes back to three things:

- Learn to love and respect yourself
- Believe that you deserve a wonderful partner
- Learn to receive and recognise good things when they come to you
- Choose to make good choices

And when we value ourselves, love ourselves, and are gentle and supportive of ourselves, then we automatically attract the wonderful people which line up with these new values.

You see, The Universe can only bring you things that are in line with the level at which you value yourself.

So say out loud: *'I know there's someone perfect for me, who makes me happy, and treats me the way I deserve to be treated… With love and respect and joy… And I can't wait to meet them'*

And feel that sense of anticipation. It's one of the most powerful ways to attract real love.

Also, you need to become proactive. Get out, do things, and meet new people. Become playful and joyful. Make your life fun and lighthearted. Fill your life with activities.

Sitting at home and expecting your perfect partner to magically appear simply will not work.

And when you meet that amazing person, please, take some advice: take things slowly! Don't throw caution to the wind and dive right in, no matter how tempting. Valuing yourself means understanding that you are a prize. And anyone who wants that prize needs to earn it.

So don't give yourself away to the first taker. If you like someone, get to know them slowly. Building a friendship is a powerful way to get to know someone before committing to a relationship.

And if someone is pressuring you to commit when you are not ready – run! There is a reason they are pushing so hard, and it usually means they are hiding their true nature or don't believe in themselves or have unresolved stuff. None of this is a good sign. You have worked hard on yourself, and you need someone who has also worked on themself. You deserve this.

Here is a great checklist for your prospective partner:

- Do they align with who you are?

- Do they have the qualities you want from a partner? (It's a great idea to make a list of the things you want in a partner.)

- Do they love you unconditionally?

- Do they accept you as you are, without wanting to try to change you?

- Are they kind, loyal and supportive?

- Are they confident in themselves?

- Do they make you feel good about yourself and life?

- Have they done the work on themselves that you have done on yourself?

- Are they financially independent and able to support themselves?

This last one is important. And it's not about the money... It's about having someone be independent so they don't expect you to support them. Having to support your partner never works – ever!

So make sure you can answer yes to each and every question above. If you have doubts, don't commit. Find someone who does meet your expectations.

Look after you. Protect your heart. Make 100% sure you give it to someone who deserves it!

Limiting belief: Unlucky in love

- **Deeper understanding:** I always attract the wrong type of person. All the good ones are taken. I'm unlucky in love.

- **Learning:** I take things slowly so that I have more control. I make good choices because I care about myself. I put myself and my happiness first.

- **Lesson:** There are many amazing people with good values looking to meet someone like me. I deserve a wonderful partner who supports and loves me.

- **New belief:** I attract the perfect partner who honours me and loves me for who I am.

I WILL NEVER AMOUNT TO ANYTHING

The number one lesson here is that you need to love what you do for a living. If you don't love your job/career/occupation, then you need to change direction. And don't think it's too late, or that you are too old! Many people change their career path late in life, myself included!

Before I switched career paths, I was an accountant: frustrated and bored with my job, feeling that I was in the wrong place doing the wrong thing. If you have that feeling too, it's time to change and expand your horizons!

We are not meant to settle... We are meant to explore our abilities and talents. So unless you are pushing yourself to the next level now, you could just as well be asleep.

Embrace new beginnings, see what you can do, and how far you can go! See how much more rewarding and fun life becomes! No dream is too big to achieve.

And don't allow fear to stop you. Yes, change is scary, but embrace that fear! It means you are on track.

A powerful way to attract promotion, opportunities, and growth, is to really love what you are doing. Embrace your career, and explore how you can expand, grow, and learn... Put in the effort and you will soon find yourself attracting awesome things and loving the process of being committed to improving your life.

Fall in love with your job/business/career; treat it as if it were a beautiful fulfilling relationship. Nurture it and love it, and grow it... Feel passion and involvement with your career... Become one with the objective of achieving great success. Get excited about achieving great things! Excitement is expectation-based, happiness based and love-based, and brings great rewards.

And use the expectation technique here too: *'I wonder what I am going to manifest today… I wonder what amazing opportunities are coming my way… I wonder what promotion is just around the corner…'*

Live it… Feel it… Breathe it… Create it…

Or, *'I wonder how it feels when I exceed my target this month… I can't wait to see my boss's face when they see the figures! I wonder what my partner / my friend is going to say when I tell them how well I've done…'*

Or if you have your own business, or want to start one, *'I wonder what amazing opportunities are on their way to me right now… I wonder what doors are going to open for me… it's going to be so interesting to see how this manifests!'*

One of my earliest clients came to see me because he was not achieving. He was in sales and wasn't reaching his targets, and was very despondent about his prospects. *'I just can't reach targets… I know I have great potential, but it's just not happening for me.'*

By the time I had seen him for a few sessions, he was a very different man!

'I had a stellar day after I saw you, and today is even better, I am feeling like an absolute rock star. I'm sticking with all of the advice you gave me and am super happy. I can't get over the difference!'

A couple of months later I heard from him again. He had been promoted to national sales manager: *'My career is skyrocketing – I can't believe how much my life has changed! I'm earning mega bucks.'*

If you feel the excitement and raise your expectations of what you can achieve, you will surprise yourself at what happens next!

Are you ready? It only gets better and better from here!

Limiting belief: I will never amount to anything

- **Deeper understanding:** I have a real fear that I am not good enough. It's safer to stay at my job. I never get noticed or rewarded. Everyone takes me for granted. I'm dull and boring and that's the way it's always been.

- **Learning:** If I put in the effort, I can achieve anything I set my mind to. I know it's going to be hard work, but it will be worth it. I'm going to prove that I know what I'm doing. My new studies/achievements fill me with confidence and excitement about the future.

- **Lesson:** I can do anything I set my mind to.

- **New belief:** The world is full of opportunities. I'm so excited to see how far I can go and how much I can achieve. I'm living my dream!

PART TWO: TWEAKING MIND AND YOUR LIFE FOR THE BEST RESULTS

A simple way to change your mind – Let go of complaining

One of the most powerful ways to take control of your mind, and your destiny, is to stop complaining and judging everything around you. We do this without even being aware of it, but we are constantly assessing everything and everyone around us.

So just stop. Stop complaining. Stop judging.

And I would challenge you to do this for two weeks, and notice the difference in the way you feel, and the peace and tranquillity you start to attract into your life.

It's a good feeling and a great basis for further work with manifesting.

Practice makes perfect – train your mind to manifest

Once you start experiencing success with some of the techniques I've been talking about, you can really play! Please understand that The Universe does not have it in for you.

It's as simple as: ***what you order is what you get.*** Once you understand that concept, you can start to play with more techniques.

Practice manifesting in your daily life – practice makes perfect!

Start practising manifesting on little things in your life.

I'll give you an example: Just yesterday I popped into a large hardware store for some items I needed. As I walked in I glanced at the queue to pay, and it was very long! I only had two small items to get, which would take just a few moments. Logically, by the time I returned, the line would be just as long, if not longer. But logic has nothing to do with manifesting and attracting what you like...

'I'd love it if the queue were really short when I got back here...' I playfully thought, *'That would be awesome!'* I quickly pictured the queue being very short when I got back. Without giving it another thought, I went inside and found my items. I was back within five minutes, and guess what? The long queue had completely disappeared! There were only two people in front of me!

Practice, practice, practice... In all sorts of ways, in all sorts of situations... Practice makes perfect. Train your mind to manifest. Practice on little things, like manifesting a great parking spot. I always drive confidently right to the entrance, secure in my expectation of the perfect parking... And there's always parking!

Teaching your mind the habit of manifesting is like training a specific set of muscles. Do it all the time, everywhere. Everything in your life is an opportunity for practice.

I even play with manifesting in my hypnosis practice. In my work life, I enjoy working with a variety of clients. What's so interesting is that I easily manifest the type of clients I want!

If I'm feeling that I want to help people achieve their goals and become great, I attract business clients who want to achieve great things.

If I get a query from a prospective client who is battling with life and has deep unresolved trauma, and I feel in my heart that I really want to help that client, nine times out of 10, that client will book with me.

So if I think, 'I'd love some more stop-smoking clients…' then boom, there are the stop-smoking clients.

It's almost like a game, and it's a really cool game because I love variety. I love working with everything, and so it's great to be able to manifest, not only plenty of clients but exactly the type of clients that I want to see.

When you play, you are training your mind, and when you train your mind, you get results!

And that's how it works.

When you get it, you get it!

When you get it, you get it! You see, once you understand how easy it is to manifest, you've got it! And once you've got it, you never forget it!

The more you play, the better the results. So, invent your own techniques… There are endless possibilities for practising manifesting!

So it's super awesome when you start playing with manifesting. You can find many ways to make your life richly rewarding… Financially, emotionally, and personally.

You do not have to 'settle' for anything! Just place your order and watch the synchronicities fall into place to bring your dreams to life in front of your eyes!

Keep It Playful And Light

Be aware of keeping it playful and light. Don't push too hard; don't try to force it. If it feels as if you are pushing a huge boulder uphill, you're doing it wrong.

I've noticed that *'forcing'* the manifesting creates intense emotions, and yes, it will bring results, but they might not be the results you were hoping for. This is because 'forcing it' is fueled by the negative emotion of desperation. And desperation is linked to fear.

So desperation, greed and demanding, are likely to result in more things to make you feel desperate, greedy and demanding. Greed cannot be satisfied, so nothing will satisfy you. Demanding is ego-driven and is likely to bring you less, not more. Good old LONA: The Law Of Negative Attraction.

Besides anything else, all negative emotions are rooted in fear. So manifesting from intensity equates to manifesting with fear.

Be mindful when you are manifesting: you are making a very simple choice: do you choose to manifest from Fear or Love?

Fear equates to greed, impatience, and desperation.

Love equates to a sense of playfulness, excitement, anticipation, trust, faith and a gentle supportive love towards yourself and the world.

Be your own observer. Watch your patterns, your lessons, your motivations, your objectives...

But the bottom line is – manifest from love and you will be blessed with abundance in all areas of your life.

Manipulating Time And Emotions For Powerfully Positive Effect

Past achievements or happy memories from the past are great ways to activate powerful states of joy and excitement. Think about the last time you achieved something that made you feel proud. Relive a beautiful memory. Feel that feeling again... The sense of accomplishment... The inner pride... The joy... The delight...

Activate those joyful feelings in your mind, your body, and your cells...

Next, shift your mind to the desire you want to manifest, and project that delight and excitement into the future. See yourself in that future, feeling that same feeling of excitement and delight AFTER you have manifested your desires...

See the events playing out in your imagination, and feel how it feels to achieve this desire... Feel it in your mind and your body, feel yourself being there, and picture the images as if you have *already* manifested this desire. Then imagine this new you, looking back at yourself now, seeing exactly what you did to make it happen!

See yourself taking the steps to create this reality, from the future! It's a bit like seeing your future but from the other side.

Imagine that new you, telling you how proud they are of you, how much fun life is now... And how grateful they are to you, for making it happen. Feel how much they love you for creating this beautiful and rewarding life...

The wonderful thing is that you have just created that *Future You* with your mind. You have just manifested your own future!

The final step in this process is to step into this new version of You, literally imagine yourself walking the walk, talking the talk.

Feel how your body moves...

What emotions do you experience?

What do you say and how do you say it?

Hear your laughter, filled with delight and joy!

The more you play with this, the sooner you will bring it into reality. Remember, your subconscious mind cannot tell the difference between what is real and what is imagined.

See yourself booking lots of clients, making huge sales, buying your own beautiful home, driving your favourite car in your favourite colour, taking those overseas trips... Imagine the joy of watching your bank balance grow... See yourself laughing and enjoying life with your perfect partner, feeling loved and appreciated... Having it all!

This is a powerful exercise to do last thing at night, just before you fall asleep, as your subconscious mind will be processing the information and actively seeking ways to make it happen! The subconscious mind is a computer processor, and its job is to find answers and bring those answers to you.

Another great time is first thing in the morning. This is a great way to start the day. Step into this new you. Walk like this you, and talk like this you... as if you already were this new you in your perfect life.

The more you play with your imagination, the more real it becomes, and the more easily the mind accepts this new reality, and naturally finds a way to make it happen… to quite literally create it and bring it into being! It's that simple!

And the best part of all is that while you are imagining being this new you, you are also boosting your self-confidence, connecting to your real self, and finding those little quirks which make you super special, super cute, and super amazing!

And that feels awesome too!

CONCLUSION:
LIFE CAN BLESS YOU BEYOND YOUR WILDEST IMAGINATION

The biggest secret to manifesting is joy. Pure, unbridled, childlike joy in living, in exploring, seeing how far you can go and how much you can achieve, and ultimately, seeing how much fun you can have with seeing how far you can go and how much you can achieve!

So, do whatever you need to do to get to that joy state. Do it now! Do it for you!

Whatever healing you need to do, do it.

Whatever counselling and therapy you need to do, do it.

Whatever courses and reading and learning you need to do, do it!

Do it and set yourself free. Because only when you have freed yourself from the past, can you manifest a brilliant future.

The subconscious mind, as powerful as it is, is wrong about one thing. Who you are and who you are capable of becoming is not based on your past.

The past does not define your future!

You are limitless. Your potential is limitless. You were born to achieve! This is your birthright! You were born to push yourself, to see how far you can go, how much you can achieve, and to explore who you are to the fullest, and beyond. This is your legacy.

So how far can you go? And how much fun can you have exploring the fullness of your beautiful and amazing spirit?

This is manifesting in its purest form.

Become you. The real you. The door is open and waiting… All you need to do is step through it and start the adventure!

You were put on this earth to learn to create these things for yourself. It's part of your life's purpose!

And the prize is abundance and joy and reward. In every aspect of your life.

I hope I have inspired you to invent some techniques of your own.

At the end of the day, you only need three things to manifest:

Playfulness, joy and imagination!

The world really is your oyster. Enjoy!

You Are Invited!

Sharon Dill offers individual coaching sessions, as well as an Abundance SuperCourse, to speed up your progress, help you overcome blocks and trauma, and shift you from the past into a beautiful and rewarding future.

Invest in yourself today and sign up now!

Visit TraumaToAbundance.com for more information.

Or contact Sharon on info@traumatoabundance.com

Learn from Sharon Dill, who has walked the walk and talked the talk, and now shares her powerful processes with the world.

Learn the advanced strategies that can lead you into abundance and joy, so that you can change your life and manifest your dreams.

Call (+27) 79 099 3252 or visit TraumaToAbundance.com

www.ingramcontent.com/pod-product-compliance
Lightning Source LLC
Chambersburg PA
CBHW052111030426
42335CB00025B/2930